CW01024217

Ukr

Voices of Resistance
and Solidarity

Ukraine
Voices of Resistance and Solidarity

Edited by Fred Leplat and Chris Ford

Resistance Books, London
and Ukraine Solidarity Campaign

Resistance Books
resistancebooks.org
info@resistancebooks.org

Ukraine Solidarity Campaign
ukrainesolidaritycampaign.org
ukrainesolidaritycampaign@gmail.com

Published 2022 by Resistance Books
and Ukraine Solidarity Campaign

Design by
Michael Wallace
Gareth Lindsay

Typefaces used
Karrik by Jean-Baptiste Morizot and Lucas Le Bihan
Cardo by David Perry

ISBN: 978-0-902869-25-7 (print)
ISBN: 978-0-902869-24-0 (e-book)

Acknowledgements

The publishers are grateful for the permission of the authors and the online journals to publish the contributions in this book. We are also grateful to Bill for checking the manuscript and making helpful suggestions. Finally, this book could not have been produced so quickly if it had not been for Michael and Gareth promptly designing the cover and the interior.

The publishers stand in solidarity with the people of Ukraine in their resistance against a brutal imperialist aggression and pay tribute to the tremendous sacrifices they have made. We support them in their fight to reconstruct their country on the basis of social and economic justice.

Contents

About the contributors

Mick Antoniw is the Labour member of the Welsh Parliament for Pontypridd, a second generation Ukrainian and trade union lawyer. He is a regular visitor to Ukraine, to Ukrainian trade unions and progressive organisations. He is a member of the Welsh Government as Counsel General and Minister for the Constitution

John-Paul Himka is a professor emeritus of History at the University of Alberta, Canada. He has written five monographs on Ukrainian history, most recently *Ukrainian Nationalists and the Holocaust*. He has also published extensively on the history of Ukrainian socialism.

Taras Bilous is a Ukrainian historian and an activist of Sotsialnyi Rukh / Social Movement. As an editor for Spilne / Commons: Journal of social critique, he covers the topics of war and nationalism.

Yuliya Yurchenko is a UK-based Ukrainian activist involved in the Ukraine Solidarity Campaign and in Ukrainian socialist organisation Sotsialnyi Rukh / Social Movement. Yuliya teaches at the University of Greenwich in London and is the author of *Ukraine and the Empire of Capital: from Marketisation to Armed Conflict*.

Oksana Dutchak is co-editor of Spilne / Commons Journal of social critique. She is a refugee in Germany with two kids and a dog, and continuing her academic work at the Berliner Institut für empirische Integrations- und Migrationsforschung.

Viktoriia Pihul is a Ukrainian feminist, anti-capitalist, and a member of Sotsialnyi Rukh / Social Movement. She is helping develop the feminist work of Social Movement. She participated in the feminist opposition platform during the uprising for democracy in Belarus.

Nataliya Levytska is Deputy Chairperson of the Confederation of Free Trade Unions of Ukraine and Deputy Chairperson of the Independent Trade Union of Miners of Ukraine and is a defender of women workers' rights.

Vitalii Dudin is President of Sotsialnyi Rukh / Social Movement. He works at the Centre for Social and Labour Research on the impact of neoliberal reforms and the social consequences of European integration. Vitalii volunteers providing legal assistance to workers.

Bogdan Ferens is a founder of the Social Democratic Platform and of Progressive Teachers., He holds a PhD in political sciences, is a public figure appearing on TV channels. His teaching focusses on political education, labour rights and social care.

Eric Toussaint is the spokesperson of the CADTM International, and sits on the Scientific Council of ATTAC France. His books include *Greece 2015: there was an alternative*; *Debt System*; and *Bankocracy*. He was the scientific coordinator of the Greek Truth Commission on Public Debt in 2015.

Ilya Budraitskis is an activist and a member of the Russian Socialist Movement. He writes regularly on politics, art, film and philosophy for openDemocracy, LeftEast, and elsewhere. He is the author of the author of *Dissidents among Dissidents: Ideology, Politics and the Left in Post-Soviet Russia*.

Niko Vorobyov is a Russian-British freelance journalist and author of the book *Dopeworld*.

Gilbert Achcar is a Lebanese socialist, a Professor of Development Studies and International Relations at the School of Oriental and African Studies. His books include *The Clash of Barbarisms: The Making of the New World Disorder; The People Want: A Radical Exploration of the Arab Uprising; and Morbid Symptoms: Relapse in the Arab Uprising*.

Simon Pirani writes at People and Nature. He is Honorary Professor in the School of Modern Languages and Cultures at the University of Durham. His books include *Change in Putin's Russia: Power Money and People*, and was the editor of the British mineworkers' union journal (1990–95).

Stephen R. Shalom and **Dan La Botz** are both socialists and editors of New Politics, an independent socialist forum for dialogue and debate on the left, based in the USA.

Introduction
Mick Antoniw

After the Second World War, the British Labour and trade union movement understandably faced many political and social challenges. In post war Britain as the Cold War developed, it largely ignored the issues around the national question in the USSR, the restriction and indeed oppression of workers' rights, the denial of human rights and the neo imperialism of the Soviet Russification policy. Russification contributed to the final collapse of the Soviet Union and the emergence of the independent states of Belarus and Ukraine.

The common narrative of many of those who supported or were sympathetic to the Soviet regime was that those who opposed or criticised it were essentially right-wing reactionaries or even Nazi sympathisers. This was the predominant message promoted successfully by Soviet propaganda which remained unchallenged in the minds of many socialists. Events in Hungary and Czechoslovakia in 1956 and 1968 changed that for many. Nevertheless, it is an ideological and cultural mind set which survives even to this day among many of those former supporters.

It is a narrative that ignores the political history of Ukraine's radical, socialist and national communist movements. At the same time it denies or seeks to rationalise what can only be described as the horror of Stalin's artificial famine which led to the death of millions of Ukrainians; the reversal of the Leninist policy of Ukrainization introduced to counter the imperialist legacy of Russian chauvinism; the thirties terror with deportations of at least hundreds of thousands of Ukrainians; and eventually Stalin's collaboration with Hitler in the 1939 pact. It is a narrative which in modern times wholly disregarded the destructive impact of decades of subsequent Russification for the nations and peoples that made up the majority of the Soviet Union.

These issues provoke many differing interpretations of domestic and geo-politics but they are all events leaving a confusing legacy that is important to disentangle.

The long tradition of radicalism in Ukrainian society, culture and literature is all but ignored within this maelstrom of conflicting politics.

Without such a proper understanding of Ukrainian history, how is anyone to fully grasp what is happening in Ukraine?

The invasion is without question a breach of international law and a crime against humanity. It has led to tens of thousands of war crimes. Despite the targeting, torture and rape of civilians witnessed internationally every day, there are still those countries and politicians who are in denial about the true and developing nature of Russia under Putin and the emergence of a new fascism, a Russian fascism.

The establishment of so-called filtration camps, concentration camps by another name, the liquidation squads and attacks on the Ukrainian language and culture are all part of a policy of genocide which is largely ignored or excused by some on the left.

In the British Labour movement there are still too many whose ill-informed or even deliberate commentary does little more than seek to appease Russian fascism. Peace at all costs, bears a remarkable similarity to the efforts in the late thirties to achieve "peace in our time" by appeasing German fascism. History repeats itself.

At the same time there are European political leaders who reject, or don't want to recognise, the importance of supporting Ukraine and the political consequences should the country fail to survive. Short term capitalist self-interest based on longer term geo-political decisions over energy dependence, trade and defence, have exposed the weakness and disunity of the European Union and international organisations such as the United Nations.

International law and the rule of law have never been under greater threat. There is a clear Russian and Chinese agenda aimed at breaking the post war consensus over the universality of such rights; ironically something they have in common with the far right in Europe and the UK Government whose own proposals for a new Bill of Rights seeks to undermine that very same principle of universality.

This lack of understanding, where it exists, also means a refusal to acknowledge that there can be no basis for peace in Ukraine while parts of it remain occupied by Russian forces. There is a failure to recognise that self-determination means the fundamental right of the Ukrainian people to decide their own future.

Another great irony emerging from this conflagration of confused ideologies and old allegiances has been the growth of a commonality of politics between elements of the socialist left, the old Stalinist left and the far right; a growing consensus which began to emerge during the Brexit referendum. Their common and shared narrative is divisive, destructive and increasingly isolated from mainstream progressive political movements in Britain and internationally.

Voices from Ukraine is a much-needed collection of progressive writings from many different perspectives, by Ukrainians about events in Ukraine leading up to and since the invasion. John-Paul Himka provides a progressive summary of Ukrainian history. Oksan Dutchak and Taras Bilous from the Ukrainian left expose the fraudulent arguments made by leftist elements against the Ukrainian resistance. Taras Bilous puts the case clearly and unequivocally that the role of socialists in Ukraine is to oppose Russian imperialism.

The role of women in the current conflict needs to be understood. As Russian troops with their government's connivance use rape and torture as weapons; as the homophobic and misogynistic policy of Russian propaganda and indeed the Russian Orthodox Church become increasingly overt, we need to listen to Ukrainian feminists such as Viktoriia Pihul.

There is a growing and vibrant trade union and labour movement in Ukraine. It includes Ukrainian miners, engineers, railway workers, teachers, health workers and many others who are at the forefront of territorial militias and civic defence. Yet there has not been a single Trades Union Congress delegation to Ukraine! Solidarity has come from trade unions individually but no trade union convoys of medical and material aid to the Ukrainian trade union movement other than those organised in conjunction with the Ukraine Solidarity Campaign.

It is only now that individual links are being formed beyond the exemplary support from the National Union of Mineworkers who have retained over the years their historic links with their fellow comrades in Ukraine.

As the war continues, as Putin becomes increasingly desperate at his failure to subdue and conquer Ukraine, the need to support the country becomes all the greater. The need for international trade union solidarity is fundamental to Ukraine's success, not just in this war, but in the reconstruction that must take place once victory is achieved. Support for the Ukrainian labour and trade union movement becomes imperative as it endeavours to protect workers' rights, develop progressive social reform and end corruption of oligarchs, government and administrations.

There will be a need to build international solidarity around a peace which guarantees Ukrainian sovereignty, democratic rights, social reform and stability.

Voices from Ukraine is a contribution to understanding what Ukrainians think, feel and need. Their voices are a call for solidarity, peace and progress. Above all this is about the Ukrainian people deciding their future and an end to Russian imperialism. For those of us on the left, whatever our differences, it is also about defeating Russian fascism.

Ten Turning Points:
A Brief History of Ukraine

John-Paul Himka

Preface

This was written as Russia's aggressive war was raging in Ukraine. I think a relatively short history of Ukraine in English, one that can be read in a couple of hours, can help people orient themselves to the issues. Every historical survey is, of course, an interpretation and a simplification. There is no way around that. I hope I have picked the most important things that need to be explained. I have included a single illustration, of the Eurasian steppe, which is in the public domain. It is easy to find historical maps on the Internet, and readers are advised to do so as required. I thank my readers Beverly Lemire, Morris Lemire, and Alan Rutkowski who have helped me prepare a more readable text. I also thank Chrystia Chomiak for formatting the text.

— *John-Paul Himka,*
  Edmonton, Alberta, March – April 2022

988

Everyone knows about the Vikings who roamed the seas. They are famous both as ferocious warriors and also as explorers of the farthest reaches of the northern hemisphere. They established short-lived settlements in North America and Greenland as well as one that survives to the present – Iceland. But there were also Vikings who roamed the rivers. They set out from Scandinavia in the ninth century, exploring the waterways that coursed through the East European forests and steppe until eventually they were able to sail to the two most magnificent and richest cities of that era, Constantinople and Baghdad. They brought goods, especially furs, to trade in Baghdad and were able to acquire luxury items that came from China via the Silk Road. They traded also in Constantinople, capital of the Byzantine empire. Here, in fact, they served the Byzantine emperor as soldiers in his Varangian Guard. 'Varangians' was how the Vikings who explored the East were called. Persons familiar with Canadian history will recognize that they were much like a medieval version of the Hudson's Bay Company.

The Varangians / Vikings established new settlements or took over existing settlements along the way, notably in Novgorod on the Volkhov River (today in Russia) and in Kyiv on the Dnipro River (today the capital of Ukraine). One Varangian leader by the name of Riuryk established a dynasty that ruled a vast realm known as Rus'. A derivative of the name Rus' has given us the English word Russia, but other derivatives, such as Rusyn or Rusnak, were ethnonyms in western territories of Ukraine into the twentieth century and up to the present.

According to the Rus' chronicle, in 988, one of Riuryk's descendents, Volodymyr (Vladimir in Russian) accepted Christianity and baptized the Rus' people. It is uncertain whether this really happened in that particular year and how it happened. The sources are too fragmentary for definitive answers. But subsequent developments make the meaning of 988 clear.

Rus' adopted Christianity from the Byzantine empire. At the time it did so, there was no division in the Christian church, no schism between East and West. But in the following centuries relations between the two large branches of Christianity deteriorated: there was a formal schism in 1054, and during the crusades Western Christians attacked the Byzantines many times, creating a wide breach between Roman Catholicism and Eastern Orthodoxy. Some historians of Ukraine have reflected that Volodymyr's was an unfortunate choice, since the West was to emerge as a global hegemon while the East was reduced to a stagnant subaltern. Perhaps.

The transition from a pagan nation into a Christian nation meant a civilizational transformation. It demanded the erection of churches. The magnificent St Sophia Cathedral, still standing on Volodymyr Street in Kyiv, was built by Volodymyr's son, Yaroslav, in the eleventh century. The rulers of Rus' and its principalities built cathedrals and churches throughout the land. Each one would require architects, engineers, and painters. At first much of this expertise had to be imported from Constantinople, but the local Rus' soon learned the requisite skills from the Byzantine masters. Things were moving fast beyond what the Viking explorers and the largely agricultural populace of Rus' could do before Christianization. The rulers also generously founded and funded monasteries. These were beacons of enlightenment in the land. The monks penned the chronicles, copied sacred texts, investigated the heavens (both theologically and astronomically), kept libraries, and produced sacral art. At the secular courts, the first Rus' law code appeared.

Crucial to the intellectual awakening of Rus' and to the development of a common culture was the adoption of writing in the Slavic language. The population of Rus' did not consist of one kind of people. There were different tribes speaking different Slavic dialects, and also peoples who spoke other tongues, including languages that were not Indo-European. In those bygone times, people did not always write in the languages they spoke. Written languages encompassed differing populations and forged commonalities. We can think of the spread of Latin across much of Europe and the spread of Arabic across the Middle East and Africa. We know that much of Rus' already spoke Slavic dialects on the eve of Christianization, but large parts of it had to be conquered linguistically and civilizationally by written Slavic.

Rus' adopted its writing system from the Byzantines' rivals, the Bulgarians. The Bulgarians wrote in a language now known as Old Church Slavonic. Texts that the Bulgarians translated from the Greek or wrote themselves were copied and sent to the monasteries and courts of Rus'. Very quickly the Bulgarian Slavonic began to adopt features of the local Rus' dialects. Certain characteristics of modern Ukrainian can be traced back to some of these early texts.

All of this civilizational development was possible because of the riches Rus' accrued as a centre of trade between the Byzantines and caliphates to the south and the Baltic regions to the north. Novgorod became part of the Hanseatic League, one of medieval Europe's richest commercial networks.

Russian and Ukrainian historians have debated whether Kyivan Rus' was Russian or Ukrainian. Most historians today consider this to be a false choice. They feel that the major events that created differentiated Russian and Ukrainian nationalities came later, after the rise of a Muscovite state and after Ukraine was incorporated into Lithuania and Poland. Old Rus' had certain things in common: a dynasty, a writing system, and a religion. There were also innumerable variations on a local scale. Rus' was like the empire of Charlemagne. The Carolingian state encompassed territories that today make up France and Germany. It was an ancestor of both French and German culture. Rus' was something akin this.

In another respect, too, Rus' was similar to the Carolingian realm. Charlemagne was able to hold his large empire together as long as he lived. So was Volodymyr. But the children and grandchildren of Charlemagne divided the lands among themselves, reducing the state to small principalities, ruled by Carolingians but no longer united. Similarly in Rus', civil war among his sons followed Volodymyr's death. And every generation afterwards divided Rus' into more and more principalities. Kyiv was no longer the capital of Rus', but the capital of the Kyiv principality. As the richest and most prestigious of the principalities, it was often attacked by rival principalities. For example, both the Galician-Volhynian principality, located in what is today western Ukraine, and the Vladimir-Suzdal principality, which eventually evolved into the Grand Duchy of Muscovy, attacked Kyiv. Attempts by the Kyivan princes to restore unity were thwarted by ambitious rivals.

1240

The internal divisions in Rus' were dangerous. To the south of the Rus' heartland was the Eurasian steppe, a large, grassy plain stretching from northeast China into central Hungary.

Horseback nomads had been crossing the steppe for millennia before Rus' was even Christianized. Some of these nomads were of Iranian stock, others Turkic. Different waves of nomads appeared at different times: Scythians, Huns, Khazars, Pechenegs (or Patzinaks), and Cumans (or Polovtsi). They sometimes raided the Rus' as they were portaging their commercial vessels along the Dnipro River. The nomads were long more of an irritant than an existential threat. In fact, during the internecine wars in Rus', the princes sometimes made alliances with the nomads against their fellow Rus'.

Then a new type of nomad appeared. A charismatic leader in Mongolia by the name of Temujin, later known as Genghis Khan, put together a huge fighting force that undertook a systematic conquest of neighbouring realms. Genghis Khan was a farsighted leader. He drafted Uighur Turks to design an alphabet and writing system for the Mongol language. He initiated written legislation. He set up an efficient postal system. Most important, he took over large parts of China in the 1220s. He recruited Chinese experts to develop his intelligence network and weaponry. The Mongols had gunpowder before any of the Europeans, including Rus'.

Several Rus' principalities as well as some of the nomads of the Ukrainian steppe first confronted the Mongols in battle in 1223. They were roundly defeated by what was essentially a Mongol scouting party. The Mongols withdrew from Rus', but learned enough about the realm and its riches to decide it was worthy of full-scale invasion. A massive Mongol army was gathered under the leadership of Genghis Khan's grandson Batu Khan. It initiated its conquest of Rus' in 1237 and reached Kyiv in 1240. The Mongols laid waste to Kyiv and its environs, reducing the Rus' capital to something like a ghost town and depopulating much of the countryside. Surviving Rus' principalities surrendered to Mongol suzerainty. Although the Mongols were ruthless in war, they understood the advantage of leaving most of their conquered populations alive in order to tax them.

But the same problem that had plagued Rus' and the Carolingian empire affected the Mongol empire. It was unable to retain unity after the death of its founder, Genghis Khan. Although the great Khan had died already in 1227, the fracturing of his empire came a few decades later; civil war among his descendants broke out in 1259. The steppe north of the Black Sea as well as the peninsula of Crimea fell under the control of the Golden Horde, one of the successors to the Mongol empire. The remnants of the Mongol army were to remain in the Rus' steppe for half a millennium. Eventually the Golden Horde became the Crimean Khanate under the suzerainty of Ottoman Turkey. Most of the 'Mongols' here were actually Turkic-speakers, descendants of the Tatar tribe that Temujin had subdued even before he was proclaimed Genghis Khan. After the Ottoman Turks took Constantinople in 1453, the Tatars of the steppe engaged in regular raids of the Slavic territories in the north to capture slaves for the Ottoman markets. After the fragmentation of the Mongols, it was possible for other regional powers to take the territories north of the steppe. Poland was able to acquire the principality of Halych, or Galicia, in the mid-fourteenth century. Around the same time, Lithuania took the nearby principality of Volhynia as well as Kyiv. The Lithuanians, whose state had not yet officially converted to Christianity, adopted the Slavonic writing system from their new subjects, the ancestors of the modern Belarusians and Ukrainians. Lithuanian princes also began to convert from their pagan cult to the Eastern Orthodox church and funded the construction of monasteries and churches.

The northeastern Rus' principality of Vladimir-Suzdal eventually moved its centre to Moscow, which became the capital of the Grand Duchy of Muscovy. Muscovy remained the longest under Mongol suzerainty, becoming fully independent only near the end of the fifteenth century. Although cultural and religious relations continued among all the Rus', the political divisions that arose after the Mongol invasion are considered by historians to be instrumental in the formation of separate Ukrainian and Belarusian nations on the one hand and Russians on the other. Historians of the early modern era generally refer to the Rus' in the Polish-Lithuanian political sphere as 'Ruthenians.' Ruthenian scholars and churchmen moved freely between Vilnius and Kyiv, creating a closely linked religious culture. But other historical processes were at work that were rapidly differentiating the Ukrainians from their Belarusian coreligionists.

1648

In the sixteenth century Spanish conquistadors subdued the Aztec and Inca empires in what for them was the New World. They looted so much silver and gold that Europe was struck by its first major inflation. Western Europe also began to develop a new economic system – capitalism. The old feudal structure, including serfdom, was breaking down. The new money and new inventions, such as the printing press, promoted what historians have often described as the Rise of the West.

Things were rather different in the eastern part of Europe. No state undertook overseas exploration. And instead of the collapse of the feudal system, a new and much more intense form of serfdom was coming into being. Beginning roughly in 1500, noble landowners throughout Poland, which at this time included Ukrainian-inhabited Galicia, began to mark off large agricultural estates for growing grain and to force the local farming population, the peasants, to work on them. The manorial estates were generally situated near a river so that the grain could be shipped to the main artery, the Vistula River, and sent downriver to the port of Gdańsk and then on to the burgeoning markets of Western Europe. It was an excellent deal for the landowners, and some noble families became so rich that they held hundreds of such estates and maintained their own armies. But it was not such a good deal for the peasants.

The enserfed peasants were expected to feed and clothe themselves from their own minor landholdings. This self-sufficiency was the major factor that differentiated their situation from that of the new kind of slaves being imported to the Americas from Africa. The serfs were tied to the land; they had no right to leave. They were taxed by their landowners, who collected money, honey, chickens, sheep, or whatever the peasants of the region produced. Mainly, however, the landlords taxed the serfs by making them perform all the labour on the manorial estate. Serfs also had a few days to work on their own plots of land. This new serfdom became more onerous as time went on. Serfs who objected to the system were beaten and imprisoned. More serious violations resulted in their execution, since nobles wielded the *jus gladii*, that is, the right to condemn their subjects to death.

The only escape from this system was to migrate to dangerous areas to the east and south, to territories where the Tatars roamed. Escaped serfs, but also adventurous nobleman, moved into the steppe, the Wild Fields as they were known back then. The migrants hunted, fished, and trapped for furs. They travelled to the Black Sea coast to collect salt for sale in the market towns of Poland and Lithuania. These frontiersmen learned to fight, since they were constantly encountering Tatar bands who wanted to sell them in the lucrative Ottoman slave market. The frontiers-men banded together at fortified locations, the most famous of which was the Zaporozhian Sich near the rapids of the Dnipro River. They came to be called Cossacks (Kozaky in Ukrainian), from a Turkish word meaning adventurer or freebooter. The Cossack heritage was a factor differentiating Ukrainians from Belarusians, although both shared the same 'Ruthenian' religious culture.

Poland and Lithuania had been joined in a personal union since the end of the fourteenth century, i.e., the King of Poland was also the Grand Duke of Lithuania. But when the dynasty that produced the joint ruler was about to die out, Poland and Lithuania agreed to a union that did not depend on dynastic ties. The Union of Lublin in 1569 created the Polish-Lithuanian Commonwealth, at that time the largest and most powerful state in the East of Europe. A provision of its terms that was to have major consequences for Ukraine was the removal of Ukraine from the Lithuanian Grand Duchy to the Polish Crown. One of its effects was that what is now Belarus and what is now most of Ukraine ended up in separate political jurisdictions.

A more significant consequence was that the Polish nobles began a concerted campaign to establish latifundia in the relatively unpopulated Ukrainian territories north of the steppe. They often enlisted the Cossacks to help them in the wars with Turkey and the Crimean Khanate that their eastward expansion provoked. The lords lured peasants from overpopulated Galicia and elsewhere to their new agricul-tural enterprises. At first the peasants were granted a period of freedom from taxation and labour duties, but after a few decades serfdom was ruthlessly imposed on the population. Again, the landlords flourished and the common people suffered. Runaway serfs joined the Cossacks, and social differences began to take on more and more of an ethnic colouring, with landlords – even if of Ruthenian origin – embracing Polish culture and Roman Catholicism while peasants and Cossacks retained the Ukrainian language, which by then was fully formed, and the Orthodox faith.

Cossack revolts and peasant revolts erupted from the end of the sixteenth century on. A major grievance of the Cossacks was the Commonwealth's policy of registration. When war broke out with Turkey and the Crimean Khanate, which happened frequently, the Cossacks would be registered and paid wages. But after a war was over, the state would reduce the number of registered Cossacks, and landlords would attempt to enserf the unregistered.

This social and military tinderbox also had a religious aspect. When the Lithuanian grand dukes first sat on the Polish throne in the late fourteenth century, they funded various Orthodox projects. But soon they adopted Roman Catholicism, and Ruthenian Orthodoxy began to be treated as a stepchild. Orthodox states neighbouring Poland-Lithuania, namely Moldavia to the south and Muscovy to the northeast, built stone monasteries and churches and funded libraries and icon-painting workshops. In Moldavia, the monasteries were both centres of learning and fortifications. In Poland-Lithuania, however, the Orthodox church was poor and its clergy relatively uneducated. The Polish state appointed laymen as bishops and as the abbots of monasteries. Laymen sought these appointments in order to collect the rents from the serfs on ecclesiastical land. Then in the sixteenth century the Reformation and the powerful Polish Catholic Counter-Reformation caught the Orthodox church off guard. Many educated Ruthenians were abandoning their native religion for Calvinism or Roman Catholicism. Desperate for an improvement in their affairs, a number of Orthodox bishops in Ukraine entered into communion with the Pope of Rome. By the terms of the Union of Brest of 1596, the Ruthenian church was allowed to retain its customary practices, such as a married clergy and the use of both wine and leavened bread in the Eucharist. The Ruthenian Orthodox who now recognized the supremacy of the pope of Rome were known as Uniates.

The church union provoked a rebellion among the monastic clergy, who rejected what their bishops had decided. This made trouble enough for the Uniate bishops in Belarus and Ukraine, but much more threatening was the repudiation of the union by the Cossacks. The defence of the ancestral Orthodox faith gave the Cossacks an ideology under whose banner they could rally. Orthodox bishops who refused to embrace the union began to look for an alliance with Muscovy, an Orthodox power that shared certain features of the old Rus' heritage.

All the tensions – social, ethnic, military, and religious – exploded into war in 1648. An angry Cossack leader, Hetman Bohdan Khmelnytsky, launched a major revolt against the Commonwealth and the nobles. Khmelnytsky was a brilliant commander and a master diplomat. He married his son to a princess of neighboring Moldavia, an Orthodox country. And in 1654 he took the fateful step of entering into alliance with the Tsardom of Muscovy. This was the first time Russia became involved in Ukrainian affairs. It never withdrew.

The war between the Commonwealth and the Cossacks was as bloody as any civil or religious war has ever been. This was an era when wounds were easily infected and impalement was a common method of execution. The Jewish inhabitants of Ukraine suffered a particular tragedy during the uprising. The Jews were rarely combatants, but many had been serving as agents of the hated manorial system. Scholars estimate that the Cossacks killed almost half of the Jewish population in the war zone.

War continued for decades thereafter, but the front stabilized in the 1670s and 1680s. The results of the conflagration marked a turning point not only in Ukrainian affairs but in the history of Eastern Europe as a whole. Until Khmelnytsky's uprising, the Polish-Lithuanian Commonwealth was the dominant power in Eastern Europe. After the uprising, Muscovy-Russia emerged on top. A century later, Poland-Lithuania ceased to exist, partitioned among Russia,

Prussia, and the Habsburg monarchy. Most of the Ukrainian-inhabited territories of the former Commonwealth were taken by Russia, but Galicia was annexed by Austria in 1772 and a part of Moldavia, soon to be known as Bukovina, was annexed shortly thereafter.

Aside from redrawing the map, the Cossack revolt had other consequences for both Ukraine and Russia. The Cossack leaders, now much enriched, endowed churches and monasteries as never before. Particularly generous was Hetman Ivan Mazepa. He funded costly decorations for churches in Ukraine and funded Orthodox projects in other countries, such as the publication of an Arab translation of the New Testament. Mazepa tried to revolt against Tsar Peter I in 1708–09 during the Great Northern War, but he failed and died in exile in Moldavia.

Kyiv had emerged as a centre of Orthodox learning already under Polish rule. In 1632 the Orthodox metropolitan of Kyiv, a Moldavian by the name of Petro Mohyla, founded a school of advanced learning that eventually became known as the Kyiv Mohyla Academy. Modelled on Jesuit colleges in Poland, it functioned much like a university. The highly educated churchmen who graduated from the academy served as bishops and teachers throughout Russia, which had nothing remotely equivalent to this institution of higher education. Ethnic Ukrainians dominated ecclesiastical and intellectual life in eighteenth century Russia. Also in Kyiv was the Kyivan Caves Monastery with its own printing press and an influential school of icon painting. The Ukrainians introduced polyphony into Orthodox music, and Ukrainians staffed the choirs at the court of the tsars and tsarinas.

1783

With its star ascendant in Eastern Europe, Russia expanded west and south. It had already managed to expand east to the Pacific by the middle of the seventeenth century. As has previously been mentioned, Poland-Lithuania was partitioned out of existence at the end of the eighteenth century (1772–95). All of what is today Belarus was joined to Russia. Russia already possessed all Ukrainian territories east of the Dnipro River. But with the partitions of Poland, it gained the territories west of the Dnipro up to the river Zbruch, its border with Austria.

In 1783, during the reign of Empress Catherine II, Russia succeeded in conquering and annexing the Crimean Khanate. This put an end to the last traces of the Mongol invasion of Rus', removed Turkish influence from the steppe, and opened the northern Black Sea coast to development. Many of the Tatars fled to what is today modern Turkey. Catherine invited colonists from abroad to settle in the underpopulated region – Germans, Greeks, Serbs, Bulgarians, and others. She also built new port cities along the coast, notably Odesa and Kherson. Most Ukrainians were enserfed and tied to the land, so originally the south had less of a Ukrainian ethnic presence than other regions of today's Ukraine.

The disappearance of both Poland-Lithuania and the Crimean Khanate made the Cossacks redundant. They were no longer useful to the Russian state. Emperor Peter I had already restricted the rights of the Cossacks, especially after Hetman Mazepa's revolt. Peter laid waste to the capital of the Cossacks' semi-state, known as the Hetmanate. Catherine, like Peter, was a modernizer and aimed at the centralization and unification of her state. Although she was never threatened by a Cossack uprising as Peter had been, she wanted Ukraine to be ruled like every other part of Russia. She dismantled all the institutions peculiar to the Hetmanate. Earlier, the territorial administration of Ukraine east of the Dnipro River had been divided into Cossack regiments. When Catherine was done, the regiments no longer existed as territorial units; instead, the former Hetmanate was divided into three gubernias, just like elsewhere in her empire.

Catherine also formally instituted serfdom, and now former Cossack officers could enserf the local population with the backing of the state. The officers aimed at assimilating into the Russian nobility and sought offices in the new state service. They spoke Ukrainian with their peasants, but among themselves they increasingly spoke and wrote in Russian.

At the end of the eighteenth century, what is today Ukraine was divided as follows. The vast majority of Ukrainian territories had now come under Russian rule. The landowners in Ukraine east of the Dnipro, known as Left-Bank Ukraine, were Russophone Ukrainians or Russians. West of the Dnipro, in Right-Bank Ukraine, the majority of the landowners were Polish. The far west had been taken by the Habsburg monarchy. In Galicia, the landlords were Polish. In Transcarpathia, the elite was Hungarian. In Bukovina, the obligations of serfdom were lighter than anywhere else, and landlords could be Romanians, Greeks, or ethnic Ukrainians. Throughout these territories, the peasantry was enserfed and, for the most part, ethnically Ukrainian.

Ukraine also contained a large Jewish minority, primarily engaged in trade, crafts, and innkeeping. Before the partitions of Poland, the Russian state did not allow Jews to settle on its territory. The Cossacks of the Hetmanate had petitioned several times to allow Jews to enter their territory, since before the uprising they had often relied on the services of Jewish merchants. The Russian emperors and empresses would not agree. However, when Catherine took Right-Bank Ukraine and Belarus from Poland, she stood before the choice of either expelling tens of thousands of Jews or making some kind of compromise. She chose the latter. Jews were allowed to enter Russia, but they were restricted to certain territories, including Ukraine. This was the Pale of Settlement. Roughly speaking, Jews made up about 12 per cent of the population in the Right Bank and about 5 per cent in the Left Bank; the south, the territory of the former Crimean Khanate, attracted many Jewish settlers, especially merchants drawn to the large trading centres of Odesa and Kherson. In Galicia, over 10 per cent of the population was also Jewish.

1861

In 1861 serfs in the Russian empire were emancipated. In many ways it was similar to the emancipation of the slaves in the USA two years later. It meant that the legal bonds of servitude were broken, but it did not mean that either the serfs or the slaves achieved meaningful equality. They remained at the bottom of the socio-economic hierarchy as well as of the cultural and educational hierarchy, and they had little or no political influence.

The first Ukrainian serfs to be emancipated were not those who lived in Russia, but the peasants who lived in the Habsburg monarchy. They were emancipated already in 1848, as one of the results of the otherwise defeated revolution of 1848 that had encompassed almost all of Europe. The plots that peasants had farmed for their own subsistence now became their legal property. Woods and forests – the commons – were divided between peasant communities and the lords, with the latter being favoured in the division.

The terms of emancipation were less favourable in Russia, and the peasants were saddled with a heavy debt to indemnify their former owners for the loss of their labour and taxes.

The same year, 1861, the national bard of Ukraine, Taras Shevchenko, passed away. He had been born a serf, but his master noticed his talent as an artist and paid for painting lessons. In 1838 a group of artists and collectors raised the funds necessary to buy his freedom, allowing him to study at the prestigious Academy of Arts in St Petersburg. Yet Shevchenko's legacy as a painter was soon eclipsed by his reputation as a poet. He published his first book of poetry in 1840, the *Kobzar* (Minstrel). These and subsequent poems electrified educated Ukrainian circles. They expressed the raw emotions of the serf class and of the nation emerging from it. Shevchenko was celebrated all over Ukraine, a frequent guest in the gentry's salons. He fell in with a group of radical Ukrainian intellectuals who dreamed of emancipating the serfs and replacing the centralized Russian autocracy with a federative democracy. This led to his arrest in 1847 and exile to a penal colony in Kazakhstan. He was allowed to return to Ukraine in 1859, but died before two years had passed, at the age of forty-seven.

This was only one of the many interesting and illustrious figures who contributed to the Ukrainian national revival of the nineteenth century. Rather than listing other prominent representatives, we offer instead a sketch of the process of the national awakening.

Ukrainians were a stateless people, hardly known outside Eastern Europe. Like many other stateless peoples, such as the Slovaks and Latvians or Scots and Welsh, they underwent a national awakening inspired by Enlightenment ideals. Educated members of these peoples, generally a rather thin stratum, began to collect the songs and stories of the common folk, to examine their fashions and write down their dialects. On the basis of this work, the intelligentsia began to compile dictionaries, forge a literary language, and define national costumes, dances, and musical instruments. The awakeners rifled through archival documents to construct a narrative of the past, a history, for their peoples, typically finding that their unknown nation dated back at least a millennium. These processes were common throughout Central and Eastern Europe in the nineteenth century, and the intellectual-cultural work grew ever more sophisticated as the century progressed. Soon organizations and political movements developed. And as faith in the old imperial order was crumbling around the turn of the twentieth century, these emerging nations began to dream of independent statehood.

Unlike most of the peoples undergoing this process, the Ukrainians were not concentrated in a single state, but were divided between the Russian empire, where most Ukrainians lived, and the Habsburg monarchy. In Imperial Russia the Ukrainian movement was initiated by the offspring of the Cossack officer class. A primary centre was in Kharkiv, where a university had been founded in 1805. Periodicals out of

Kharkiv, like *The Ukrainian Herald* and *The Ukrainian Journal*, promoted Cossack history and popularized the term 'Ukraine,' which had been used by Khmelnytsky earlier. A university was also founded in Kyiv in 1834, and this city emerged as the centre of the Ukrainian movement as of the 1840s. But the movement's development in Russia was severely handicapped. Publication in the Ukrainian language was restricted, nearly banned, by decrees of 1863 and 1876. Leaders of the movement were arrested or forced into exile. The tsarist regime did not develop a comprehensive system of primary education, and the schools that existed were prohibited from using the Ukrainian language in the classroom. These circumstances, combined with the lack of basic civil rights in Russia, such as freedom of the press and freedom of association, prevented the Ukrainian movement from making much of an impact on the vast majority of ethnic Ukrainians, namely the peasants. In Russia, the Ukrainian movement was top heavy, composed of outstanding visionary intellectuals who lacked a social base. The first Ukrainian political party in the empire was the underground Revolutionary Ukrainian Party, founded in 1900. Like the movement that produced it, it combined social justice concerns with national goals. It also issued a brochure calling for an independent Ukraine.

Three Ukrainian-inhabited regions existed in the Habsburg monarchy: formerly Polish Galicia, formerly Moldavian Bukovina, and Transcarpathia, which had been part of Hungary since about 900. The awakener stratum here was not of Cossack origin, but clerical. Galicia and Transcarpathia had accepted the Uniate faith in the late seventeenth century. (Uniatism disappeared completely from the Russian empire by the mid-1870s.) The enlightened Habsburg empress Maria Theresa made a number of improvements in the affairs of the Ukrainian population. Symbolically, she renamed the Uniate church the Greek Catholic rite to emphasize its parity, in her eyes, with the Roman Catholic rite. She also instituted higher education for the

Greek Catholic parish clergy, who had not been provisioned with such before. Eventually, Greek Catholic seminarians were to study at Lviv University, which had been founded in 1661. These educated priests, and later their sons, served as the awakeners and leaders of the national movement in the monarchy. The Ukrainians of all social classes here called themselves Rusyns (or Ruthenians) rather than Ukrainian. The latter name did not become dominant in these western regions until about 1900.

The European revolution of 1848 first brought the Ruthenians into politics and saw the appearance of the first newspaper in a variety of the Ruthenian language. There were arguments for many decades about what language the Galician Rusyns should write in – in local dialects mixed with Church Slavonic or in Russian or in the Ukrainian literary language that had developed among the Ukrainian intelligentsia of the Russian empire. The debate over language was a debate also over identity. Were they simply Rusyns or a branch of the Russian nation or a branch of the Ukrainian nation? The Galicians and, with somewhat of a lag, the Bukovinians, opted for Ukrainian identity by the end of the century, while the Ruthenians in Transcarpathia remained divided. When Austria introduced a constitution, a limited suffrage, and civil freedoms in 1867, the fortunes of the Ukrainian movement in Galicia rose rapidly. Numerous periodicals appeared and created the 'imagined community' of a nation across villages and towns. Public primary education was introduced in 1869 and the language of instruction in eastern Galicia, where the Ruthenians lived, was Ukrainian. The intelligentsia in Lviv and the network of clergy in the countryside founded numerous organizations for the peasantry – choirs, fire brigades, cooperatives, and adult education societies. The first Ukrainian political party in Austria was founded in 1890, the agrarian socialist Radical Party. By the late 1890s young Radicals were formulating a programme calling for an independent Ukrainian state. Also, members of the Radical Party broke off to form the

Ukrainian National Democratic Party, a left-liberal party that would dominate Galician-Ukrainian politics until 1939, and the Ukrainian Social Democratic Party, a workers' party linked with the Austromarxists. In the early 1900s all these parties supported a series of agricultural strikes, seeking to raise the wages of the poorest Ukrainian peasants. The mood in late-nineteenth century Galicia was well captured by the poet Ivan Franko: 'I am a son of the people, the son of a nation on the rise. I am a peasant: prologue, not epilogue.'

1917

By the eve of World War I, mighty changes were brewing in the Russian empire. In 1905 the First Russian Revolution broke out. New political parties emerged from the shell of the Revolutionary Ukrainian Party – two Ukrainian Social Democratic parties and the more nationalistic Ukrainian People's Party. The tsarist autocracy was forced to make a number of liberal concessions, including the right to publish in the Ukrainian language. Many Ukrainian newspapers and journals appeared overnight as did Ukrainian civic organizations. Russian imperial society was deeply polarized between reaction and revolution. Ukrainians, like other groups that were discriminated against under tsarism, such as the Jews, sided with the revolution. But the tsar and forces of reaction were able to push back against the liberal concessions that had been made, so that the Ukrainian movement was not able to make the kind of progress it would have done, had Russia evolved toward democracy instead.

And even this relatively liberal period in the history of Russia was cut short by the outbreak of World War I in 1914. The front moved back and forth across Ukraine: in 1915 the Russians were in Lviv and in 1918 the Germans were in Kyiv. This new industrial war took many lives and devastated the infrastructure across Ukrainian territories.

Russia was in many ways the weakest of the powers engaged in the war. It lagged behind the rest of Europe in industrial development, it was plagued with social tensions, and its soldiery was the least educated of any of the fighting forces. The strain on the population led to spontaneous outbreaks of protest, ultimately forcing the tsar to abdicate in March 1917.

The revolution gave newfound life to the Ukrainian movement. As councils or soviets popped up all over Russia, Ukrainians in Kyiv founded their own, the Ukrainian Central Rada (Rada in Ukrainian is the equivalent of soviet). The Rada, the Ukrainian revolutionary parliament, was dominated by social democrats and peasant-oriented socialist revolutionaries. It sought recognition and autonomy from the Provisional Government, which claimed to be in charge of all of Russia. At one point in this struggle, the Rada proclaimed the existence of the Ukrainian People's Republic; this was not envisioned as a totally independent state, but part of a democratic Russian federation. But while the Rada was tussling with the Provisional Government, the latter was overthrown by the Bolsheviks in November 1917. The Rada considered the Bolsheviks to be extremists creating chaos in the former empire, and the Bolsheviks considered the Rada to be petty bourgeois and nationalist.

In December 1917 the Bolsheviks attacked the Rada militarily. The forces of the Ukrainian People's Republic were not able to defend their territory, and the Rada called upon the Germans to rescue them. World War I was still proceeding, and the Germans looked to Ukraine as a source of food and raw materials and as a buffer state against Russia, with whom they were still at war. German expropriations led to peasant revolts. After the Germans' defeat by the Entente and their withdrawal from Ukraine, things became ever more complicated. The Ukrainian forces fought the Bolsheviks as well as the White Russian generals of the civil war. They met with little success. The army, headed by Symon Petliura, was undisciplined, and units associated with it engaged in bloody pogroms against the Jewish population, resulting in tens of thousands of deaths. New forces kept entering the fray – warlords, the most famous of whom was the anarchist Nestor Makhno; a French expeditionary force; and the Polish army under the leadership of Józef Piłsudski. The Ukrainian Galician Army also joined Petliura's forces in summer 1919; these were disciplined, experienced soldiers, but they could do little to improve Ukrainians' fortunes.

The Ukrainian Galician Army had been the armed force of the western Ukrainian People's Republic. That republic had been proclaimed in Lviv on 1 November 1918, as Austria-Hungary was collapsing under the impact of defeat in war. The Ukrainians lost Lviv in a matter of weeks, since – as in most cities on Ukrainian territories – only a minority of its inhabitants were ethnically Ukrainian. The Poles in the city succeeded in forcing the Ukrainian government out. The Jewish population tried to remain neutral during the conflict in Lviv, but the Poles suspected them of favouring the Ukrainians. As a result, Polish soldiers and the urban crowd unleashed a pogrom. The Ukrainian People's Republic was not yet defeated and held most of eastern Galicia until June 1919. They were only forced to leave these territories when a Polish army, equipped and trained by the French to fight against the Bolsheviks, over-whelmed them. That is how and why the Ukrainian Galician Army joined with Petliura's forces to the east.

Ukraine experienced six terrible years of war and civil war before things settled down. In the early 1920s, the territory of what is today modern Ukraine was divided among a number of states. Most of Ukraine became the Ukrainian Soviet Socialist Republic. Crimea, however, was part of Soviet Russia. Since Hungary was defeated in the war and stripped of most of its historical territories, Transcarpathia was assigned to the newly created state of Czechoslovakia. Bukovina was incorporated into Romania. And Galicia, which had been part of Austria, as well as Volhynia, which was just to the north of it and had been part of Russia, were incorporated into the new Polish state. The failure to establish their own state, at a time when long-dead states such as Poland and Lithuania were resurrected and entirely new states such as Finland and Czechslovakia were created, was to be a source of great bitterness and frustration for Ukrainians.

The only flicker of a candle in the national darkness was Soviet Ukraine. In Lenin's view, the Ukrainian forces may have been defeated, but not the Ukrainians' national aspirations. He therefore, against the will of many other leading Bolsheviks, insisted on the creation of a Ukrainian Soviet republic, roughly in the borders that had been claimed by the Central Rada. In line with Lenin's policies, the Bolsheviks in 1923 adopted a policy of indigenization (*korenizatsiia*) in the non-Russian Soviet republics. This policy resulted in an unprecedented blossoming of Ukrainian culture. During Ukrainization, as the indigenization policy was known in Soviet Ukraine, Ukrainians devised a unique educational system; produced avantgarde cinema, theatre, literature, and visual art; and undertook extensive research on Ukrainian history and culture. This was the era of Ukrainian national communism, when ethnic Ukrainians were appointed to leading positions in the political and economic apparatus. Ukrainians from Poland, who were discriminated against, migrated to Soviet Ukraine to work in encyclopaedia projects and many other cultural endeavours.

In Poland, the Ukrainian educational system that had existed under old Austria was dismantled. Ukrainians were not hired for state jobs, such as in the railways or local administration. They began to develop a state within a state, funding private Ukrainian educational opportunities and cultural work with funds provided by the Ukrainian cooperative movement. The Greek Catholic church founded a theological academy which actually trained numerous secular intellectuals, since access to university education was limited for Ukrainians, as it was for Jews, in interwar Poland. The catalogue of Poland's discriminatory policies against national minorities is long.

Politically, the dominant party was the Ukrainian National Democratic Alliance, whose name accurately reflected its politics. There were also left-wing parties, ranging from the fairly moderate Ukrainian Radical Party to the Communist Party of Western Ukraine. In between were the Social Democrats, some of whom were pro-Bolshevik. In the 1920s pro-Soviet attitudes were widespread in Galicia because of what was happening in national communist Soviet Ukraine. There was also a strong women's movement allied with the National Democrats.

On the right of the political spectrum was the Ukrainian Military Organization, known by its Ukrainian initials UVO. It continued a struggle against Polish rule from the underground, robbing post offices and engaging in other forms of terrorism. In 1929 many in UVO joined the newly founded Organization of Ukrainian Nationalists (OUN). OUN also engaged in robberies and assassinations. During their summer vacation in 1930 the youth of OUN and UVO launched a campaign of arson against Polish estates and undertook other forms of sabotage. The Polish government responded with a vicious pacification of the Ukrainian countryside, beating Ukrainian activists of all political stripes and destroying buildings belonging to the Ukrainian movement. It was a brutal overreaction, and Ukrainians at home and in North America called upon the international community to condemn Poland.

1933

In 1933 the policy of Ukrainization was officially ended in Soviet Ukraine. But before that, in 1930, numerous Ukrainian cultural and academic workers were arrested and put on trial for belonging to a fictitious Union for the Liberation of Ukraine. Vicious purges of the Ukrainian intellectual elite marked the entire 1930s. Few survived. In 1933 the minister of education in Soviet Ukraine, Mykola Skrypnyk, and the proletarian writer Mykola Khvyliovy committed suicide in protest.

Aside from the Stalinist terror, Ukraine suffered immensely from forced collectivization. The planning and implementation of collectivization were abysmally poor, and food shortages haunted the entire USSR. Famine broke out in Kazakhstan, the Volga region, and Ukraine. The manmade famine in Ukraine, the height of which came in 1933, took 4 million lives out of a total population of about 31.5 million. The effects of the collectivization famine were most intense in Ukraine. Numerous witnesses related that even small amounts of food were taken from individual households, leaving the inhabitants to starve. Because the famine occurred at the same time as Stalin was also persecuting the Ukrainian elite, which he considered disloyal, the deadly effects of food shortages throughout the USSR were disproportionately displaced to Ukraine.

The purges and famine in Soviet Ukraine put an end to all pro-Soviet sympathies in the western Ukrainian regions outside Stalin's reach.

Most of Europe in the 1930s was polarized between left and right, between the communists and the fascists. Street fights between left and right paramilitaries broke out in Vienna, and Spain, of course, was plunged into civil war. Democracy on the continent was weak. In 1933 Hitler came to power in Germany. He made no secret of his hatred for Jews and his plans to undo the terms of the peace settlement imposed on Germany after defeat in World War I. In his book *Mein Kampf* Hitler developed his racist visions and announced for all the world to read his intent to seek *Lebensraum* (living space) for Germans by invading the Soviet state.

Hitler exercised a baleful influence on the Ukrainian right in Poland, particularly the OUN. The Nationalists had already been spying for and accepting aid from Germany before the Nazis took it over. But now the Nationalists' orientation towards Germany became stronger. Hitler was the enemy of their enemies, the Soviet Union and Poland. Hitler was revising the same Versailles settlement that had left Ukrainians stateless.

He was uniting the German people that had previously lived in different states: he annexed Austria in March 1938 and the so-called Sudetenland of Czechoslovakia in October of that year. As a result of the latter annexation, what had been Czechoslovakia began to break down into separate units. One of these was Carpatho-Ukraine, formed from some of the Rusyn / Ukrainian-inhabited territory of Czechoslovakia. Ukrainians outside the Soviet Union, in Galicia and North America, were ecstatic about the formation of this statelet. OUN sent its militants to Carpatho-Ukraine to influence its administration and to join its nascent armed force. When Hungary attacked and put an end to Carpatho-Ukraine in mid-March 1939, some leading cadres of OUN perished in the struggle for Carpatho-Ukraine's independence. There was some ideological overlap between OUN and German national socialism from the beginning, and as the 1930s progressed the Nazis' influence on Nationalist ideology increased. Particularly noticeable was the growth of antisemitism in the OUN during the latter 1930s.

1939

World War II broke out on 1 September 1939. Shortly before, Germany and the Soviet Union signed a non-aggression pact. A secret codicil of the pact was a division of Eastern Europe between the two powerful dictatorships. On 17 September the Soviets invaded Western Ukraine, i.e., Galicia and Volhynia in Poland, and in a matter of weeks annexed it to the Soviet Union. The twenty-one months that the Soviets occupied Western Ukraine were brutal. Hundreds of thousands of people were deported to the Arctic, Kazakhstan, and Siberia. At first the Soviets arrested and deported the Polish elite of Eastern Poland / Western Ukraine. They also dispatched to the Gulag Jews who fled from the German zone of Poland to the Soviet zone. And near the end of the occupation, the prisons were filled with Ukrainians. The Soviets also took Bukovina from Romania in June 1940, subjecting it to the same type of regime.

During the Soviet occupation, life changed dramatically. What was once a diverse array of periodicals and newspapers was now replaced by repetitive mouthpieces of the new authorities. Basic provisions disappeared from the stores. Stores and businesses were nationalized. All the basic civil rights that had existed even under authoritarian Poland were swept away. Fear pervaded the population, as at any moment literally anyone could end up on a freight car to Siberia. All the preexisting Ukrainian political parties dissolved themselves soon after the Soviets took power. They were never to revive their activities. The Soviets hunted down and executed dissident communists in Western Ukraine, national communists and left communists. There was only one Ukrainian political movement that managed to survive the Soviet period – the OUN. It had experience in conspiratorial activity, and – despite arrests and executions at the hands of the authorities – managed to double its membership. In June 1941, the organization had about 20,000 members and 30,000 sympathizers. If years of underground experience allowed the OUN to survive, the repressive Soviet system drove some Ukrainians, especially youth, into its ranks.

On 22 June 1941, Hitler launched his ill-fated invasion of the Soviet Union. In the days before the Germans were able to reach Western Ukraine, the Soviet secret police, the NKVD, arrested thousands of suspected Ukrainian Nationalists, lest they aid the enemy. Then, since the German advance was so rapid, they were unable to evacuate the prisoners to the east. Instead, they executed them *en masse*, killing about 15,000 in Western Ukraine, mainly Ukrainians, but also Poles and Jews. These NKVD murders enraged the population of Western Ukraine, raising emotions to a very high pitch. When the Germans arrived, Jews were forced to retrieve the victims' bodies from the prisons and lay them out in the courtyards for people to find their relatives. Parts of the city of Lviv stank from the decomposing bodies. A pogrom broke out in which the Ukrainian National Militia of the OUN played a major role, although the German SS was responsible for executing most of the hundreds of victims. Violence against Jews continued throughout the war. About 1.5 million Jews were killed on the territory of today's Ukraine, accounting for about a quarter of the victims of the Holocaust. Most Jews died not far from where they had lived, shot on the edge of ravines or pits dug for the purpose. The shooters were primarily special SS units, the Einsatzgruppen, aided, however, by the collaborationist police.

Nazi policy towards the local non-Jewish population was also harsh, though it stopped short of systematic mass murder. Over 3 million Soviet prisoners of war died in German camps from exposure and starvation. Over 2 million young Ukrainians were deported to Germany as slave labourers (*Ostarbeiter*). In much of Ukraine, the Germans rounded up youth as they came out of church or a dance and packed them on to trains.

What is today Ukraine was divided among a number of different administrations during the war. Galicia was incorporated into the rump Poland, the General Government, as Distrikt Galizien. Bukovina and neighbouring regions were reannexed by Romania, which also took the Odesa region and called it Transnistria. Hungary held Transcarpathia / Carpatho-Ukraine. Parts of Ukraine were under direct German military rule. The largest part of dismembered Ukraine was the Reichskommissariat Ukraine.

The most savage of these administrations was the Reichskommissariat, which had its capital in Rivne in Volhynia. Although the OUN had been cooperating with the Nazi occupation as policemen in Volhynia, it realized that the population was fed up with German rule and engaging in spontaneous acts of resistance. Rather than let the anti-German sentiments feed into support for the Red partisans who were coming through the forests, the OUN launched its own anti-German insurgency in the spring of 1943. It was a limited resistance movement, since the OUN did not want a Soviet victory either. The OUN armed force, the Ukrainian Insurgent Army (UPA), ambushed German patrols and interfered with round-ups for slave labour, but it did not try to derail German trains carrying supplies to the front. It preferred the Germans and Soviets to pummel each other. The UPA resistance did not do anything to protect the Jewish population hiding in the woods of Volhynia; in fact, it issued an order to kill all Jews and any Ukrainians who hid them. The UPA also began to ethnically cleanse Volhynia, and afterwards Galicia, of its Polish population. Historians estimate that the UPA killed about 60,000 Poles, for the most part civilians.

The war in Ukraine was extremely brutal. In Eastern Europe the conflict was not between the Western Allies and the Germans but between the Soviets and the Germans, i.e. between two lethal regimes. People had to make choices. Generally, the population of the Reichskommissariat Ukraine tended to look at the advancing Red Army as liberators. But this was much less the case in Distrikt Galizien in Western Ukraine. The experience of Soviet rule in 1939–41 hardened attitudes. Also, German rule here was much more favourable to Ukrainians than anywhere else on Ukrainian-inhabited territory. The Germans used the Ukrainians as a counterweight to the Poles and relied on Ukrainian Nationalists to help set up the civil administration and police. Recruitment of slave labour also existed here, but there were certain mitigating factors that did not obtain elsewhere. Educational opportunities for Ukrainians existed in Distrikt Galizien that had no equivalent in the Reichskommissariat. Because of Nationalist influence, the Ukrainians of Galicia were less horrified by the murder of the Jewish population than were Ukrainians in the Reichskommissariat. In fact, the liquidation of the Jewish population proved to be an economic boon for the Ukrainian cooperative movement during the war. The Germans had enough popularity in Galicia in mid-1943 and 1944 for 80,000 Ukrainians to volunteer for a Waffen-SS unit, the Division Galizien. Only a portion of these volunteers actually ended up fighting. Waffen-ss Division Galizien played a very minor role in anti-Jewish and anti-Polish actions, but it collaborated in quelling the antifascist Slovak National Uprising in 1944.

After the Soviet reconquista of Western Ukraine, the UPA ignited an anti-Soviet insurgency, which lasted into the late 1940s. The Soviet counter-insurgency was ruthless. Dead UPA soldiers were lined up against the fence in villages, so that relatives could identify them. If anyone did admit to finding their son or brother among the dead, they would be arrested and sent to labour camps. Hundreds of thousands of Western Ukrainians were deported as part of the counter-insurgency and in connection with the collectivization drive.

A result of this history, which was to play a role in the memory politics of independent Ukraine, was that Galician Ukrainians remembered the Soviets as worse than the Germans, while in the rest of Ukraine the tendency was rather the other way around.

One result of the war for all of Eastern Europe was that states became ethnically more homogenous. The Germans had killed most of the Jews. All East European countries expelled their ethnic German population. In Ukraine, the Polish population largely disappeared. Many had been killed in the Stalinist purges of the 1930; large numbers of them were deported from Western Ukraine in 1939–41; the UPA ethnic cleansing campaign eliminated tens of thousands more in 1943–4; and after the war, the Soviets organized population exchanges with Poland, trading surviving Poles for Ukrainians who had ended up within the new People's Poland. Jews who managed to survive the war generally left Western Ukraine for Poland, and then for Israel and America. The former Jewish population of Ukraine, with its religious traditions and its Yiddish language, existed no more. Such Jews as remained in Ukraine were indistinguishable from other Soviet citizens. Russian replaced Yiddish.

The absence of Poles and Jews opened up many towns and cities in Western Ukraine for ethnic Ukrainian migrants. This was a major social advance for the Western Ukrainian population, although they had to compete with incoming Russians and Russophone Ukrainians from the East. The latter formed the political elite throughout Ukraine.

After Stalin died, the Soviet Union became a much safer place to live. Many of the Western Ukrainians in the Gulag were amnestied and returned home. There were brief moments of thaw in regard to Ukrainian culture, all concentrated in the period 1956–72. Otherwise, the postwar period in Soviet Ukraine witnessed relentless russification. Those who objected were arrested and imprisoned or exiled. These were the dissidents, and they represented various shades of political opinion, from Marxists like Ivan Dziuba and Leonid Pliushch to Nationalists like Valentyn Moroz and Ivan Kandyba. Composers, poets, and artists were also associated with the dissident milieu.

The Ukrainian Soviet Socialist Republic that emerged from the war encompassed not only the old, pre-1939 Soviet Ukraine but the territories Stalin took in 1939–41, i.e., Galicia (basically Lviv, Ivano-Frankivsk, and Ternopil oblasts), Volhynia (basically Rivne and Volhynia oblasts), and Bukovina (basically Chernivtsi oblast). In addition, Soviet Ukraine added Transcarpathia oblast in 1945, when it was ceded by Czechoslovakia. (The twenty-four oblasts of Ukraine are the equivalent of states or provinces.) The last addition to Soviet Ukrainian territory was Crimea, transferred from the Russian SFSR to the Ukrainian SSR in 1954. The year 1954 was the 300th anniversary of the Treaty of Pereiaslav, by which Hetman Bohdan Khmelnytsky placed Ukraine under the protection of the Russian tsar.

1991

The 1970s and first half of the 1980s in the Soviet Union have been called 'the period of stagnation'. The USSR was plagued with an aging and unwell leadership. Communist Party general secretary Leonid Brezhnev had been born in 1906. He was a heavy smoker and drinker, and his health declined dramatically by the mid-1970s. After his death in 1982, he was succeeded by two more elderly general secretaries, both of whom were dead by spring 1985. The Communist Party then chose a younger man as general secretary, Mikhail Gorbachev, hoping he would breathe new life into the party and the country. Gorbachev promised liberal reforms, whose slogans were *perestroika* (reconstruction) and *glasnost* (openness). The reforms he initiated were eventually to lead to the end of communism in Europe and the dissolution of the Soviet Union.

The reforms reached Kyiv more slowly than other major Soviet centres. The head of the Communist Party of Ukraine, Volodymyr Shcherbytsky, was a fossil of the stagnation period. He came to power in 1972, inaugurating his tenure as Soviet Ukraine's first secretary by a massive arrest of dissidents and a clampdown on Ukrainian culture and scholarship. He kept a tight grip on Ukraine as long as he could. In 1986 an explosion occurred at the Chornobyl nuclear power plant, the worst nuclear accident in history. Shcherbytsky tried to hush it up and did not even cancel the May Day parade in Kyiv that took place only five days later. His handling of this crisis provoked denunciations at the June 1986 conference of the Ukrainian Writers' Union. Ivan Drach, whose son was sent to clean up at Chornobyl and was poisoned by radiation, was particularly outspoken. Writers at the congress also called for more Ukrainian cultural autonomy.

Changes in Ukraine began to accelerate after numerous dissidents were released by the all-Union government from prison and exile and returned to Kyiv and Lviv in 1988–89. In early 1989 the dissidents now at liberty joined with the writers to form a movement to press for Ukrainian rights. It was called the People's Movement of Ukraine for Reconstruction, popularly known as Rukh. Rukh issued a democratic programme advocating a civic Ukrainian nation, i.e., one not limited to ethnic Ukrainians or Ukrainian-speakers but comprising all inhabitants of the Ukrainian republic. Before long it was advocating the independence of Ukraine from the Soviet Union.

Strivings for independence on the part of the Ukrainian public came at a propitious moment. Just then, a new figure was coming to prominence, Boris Yeltsin. He challenged Gorbachev, who was becoming more conservative in reaction to the forces his reforms had unleashed, not just in Ukraine but in Lithuania, Armenia, and other republics. Gorbachev wanted to preserve the unity of the Soviet Union. Yeltsin attacked Gorbachev not from the all-Union level, but from the level of the Russian republic. He became chair of the Russian Supreme Soviet in 1990, which signified he was head of state in Russia. He made alliances with the republican level of leadership outside Russia, and in particular with the communists of the Ukrainian republic. Yeltsin pushed through a declaration of sovereignty for Russia on 12 June 1990, and Ukraine followed suit on 16 July. The declaration of state sovereignty of Ukraine was so far-reaching that when Ukraine actually became independent, on 24 August 1991, the declaration of independence was less than 100 words long and contented itself with proclaiming it was fulfilling the terms of the sovereignty declaration. Ukraine's equivalent of Yeltsin was Leonid Kravchuk; a week after the promulgation of sovereignty he was elected chair of Ukraine's Supreme Soviet, better known by its Ukrainian name – the Verkhovna Rada. Kravchuk developed good relations with Rukh and also with Yeltsin. Both communist leaders wanted to dissolve the Soviet Union, and they realized their goal in December 1991.

The declaration of independence was preceded by a clumsy coup attempt by Kremlin hardliners on 19–23 August 1991. Yeltsin became a hero in Russia for opposing the coup. Ukrainian communists were not sure what to do, but the day after the coup failed, the Verkhovna Rada declared independence. Independence was to be confirmed by a referendum of the population of Ukraine. It took place on 1 December and resulted in a majority vote for independence. However, it was not entirely like the elections Ukraine was to have later. Soviet-style practices were still in evidence, with some electoral districts reporting that 99.9 or 100 per cent of the eligible voters took part, of whom over 97 per cent were in favour of independence. Nonetheless, the referendum dotted the 'i' on the word independence.

On the same day as the referendum Ukraine held its first presidential election. Kravchuk won handily, with over 60 per cent of the vote. Already in evidence was the regional voting pattern that marked almost every election in independent Ukraine: the West voted one way, the South and East another way.

Concretely, Kravchuk in 1991 won every oblast in Ukraine except for the three Galician oblasts. In the 1994 elections the western half of the country voted unsuccessfully to re-elect Kravchuk, but the rest of the country voted for Leonid Kuchma from Dnipro (at that time Dnipropetrovsk) in south-central Ukraine. In 1999 Kuchma ran against the communist Petro Symonenko. The three Galician oblasts voted over 90 per cent in favour of Kuchma, while Symonenko did well in northcentral Ukraine, Donetsk and Kherson oblasts, and Crimea. In the 2004 elections, which sparked the Orange Revolution, former head of the national bank and prime minister Viktor Yushchenko won, taking the entirety of West and Central Ukraine. His opponent Viktor Yanukovych of Donetsk took the South and East. In the next election, Yanukovych won against former prime minister Yuliia Tymoshenko. Yanukovych again took the South and East.

This voting pattern reflected different historical experiences that led to different attitudes toward Ukrainian ethnonationalism and toward Russians. The West was solidly in the nationalist camp, which soon captured the Centre as well. The largely Russophone East and South was less anti-Russian.

Galician Ukrainians and Ukrainians from Donetsk or Odesa were only slowly building their solidarity.

The 1990s were very hard on the Ukrainian population. Inflation reached unheard of heights. A life's savings in roubles might only be worth enough to buy a pack of matches. Where possible, many urban Ukrainians went to their families in the countryside to help on the farms and bring home a bag of potatoes. But some people became very rich as what had been state property was privatized. Common schemes in the 1990s included paying people Soviet wages and selling their products to Europe at Western prices; taking loans from the banks in Ukrainian currency, changing them into American dollars, and somewhat later paying the loans back in devalued Ukrainian currency; stripping existing state enterprises of their assets and selling them; and clear-cutting forests and selling the lumber abroad for hard currency. As a result of the latter practice, Transcarpathia was wracked by floods. Racketeers collected protection payments from nascent retail businesses. Business and organized crime were often indistinguishable There arose in Ukraine a stratum of very rich and powerful businessmen, usually called the oligarchs. Prominent among them were Viktor Pinchuk and Rinat Akhmetov. Such figures retain great influence behind the scenes in Ukrainian politics. The economic crisis of the 1990s began to abate after autumn 1996 when the currency was reformed and the *hryvnia* introduced to replace earlier forms of Ukrainian currency.

It is important to mention something that did not happen. Although Romania, the former Soviet republics on the Baltic, and other countries of post-communist Eastern Europe were taken into the European Union in the 2000s, Ukraine was excluded. Things could have turned out quite differently if it had been otherwise.

2014

There was a prelude to the 2014 events, namely the Orange Revolution. The 2004 election was contested, as already mentioned, between two Viktors, Viktor Yushchenko and Viktor Yanukovych. The latter, who was prime minister at the time, had the support of the Ukrainian government and was also the candidate favoured by Russian president Vladimir Putin. Yushchenko, an opposition leader, was considered a pro-Western candidate. Yanukovych won the run-off election between the two, by a fairly narrow margin (49.5 per cent to 46.6 per cent). Yushchenko's supporters claimed that the election results had been falsified, and a large crowd from all over Ukraine occupied Independence Square, known as Maidan Nezalezhnosti in Ukrainian. Perhaps half a million protesters gathered on the Maidan, in the heart of downtown Kyiv. A stage was erected on the square, and opposition figures gave speeches and popular rock groups played music. Kyivans brought food to the protesters. Western media and politicians also supported the demonstrators and their Orange Revolution. Under pressure from the crowd, a new run-off election was held, but this time observers from other countries were stationed at polling booths to make sure that the voting was fair. When the votes were tallied, Yushchenko proved to be the victor (52.0 per cent to 44.2 per cent).

Yushchenko was not an effective president, and his term was marked by quarrels with other politicians who had gained prominence during the Orange Revolution, notably Yuliia Tymoshenko. In 2008 Yushchenko even appointed his former electoral opponent, Yanukovych, as prime minister. The major innovations of his term as president were in the realm of memory politics. Unlike any Ukrainian president before him, he initiated not only the rehabilitation of the OUN and the UPA, but their glorification. He posthumously awarded their leaders, particularly Roman Shukhevych (Supreme Commander of the UPA) and Stepan Bandera (head of the largest faction of the OUN), the honour of Hero of Ukraine. He also led a massive campaign to have the man-made famine of 1932–33, the Holodomor, recognized by all other countries as a genocide directed against the Ukrainian people. He ordered the collection of over 200,000 testimonies about the famine and founded a memorial museum in Kyiv to commemorate the victims.

Yushchenko did not even make it to the run off in the presidential elections of 2010. Instead, Tymoshenko faced off with Yanukovych, who won, 49 to 45.5 per cent. The victory of Yanukovych was a victory for his clan in Donetsk, who occupied influential positions in his government. He made an about-face from Yushchenko's nationalist politics, and his minister of education and science, Dmytro Tabachnyk, alienated many Ukrainian intellectuals. Yanukovych was also the most corrupt of the Ukrainian presidents. He and his cronies embezzled in an ostentatious manner. Yanukovych remained popular in his base in the Donbas, but much of Ukraine felt he was a disgrace to the presidency.

The writing on the wall appeared in November 2013. Yanukovych was supposed to sign a political association and free trade agreement with the European Union but instead accepted financial aid from Russia. Once again, the Maidan began to fill with protesters, eventually half a million of them. They were a mixed bunch. Although the Galicians were disproportionately represented, protesters came from all parts of Ukraine. Some were pro-Western democrats, some were far-right nationalists; feminists, members of the LGBT community, anarchists, and socialists were also there. Yanukovych's government reacted with lethal violence against the protesters, and the nationalists – led by Right Sector – fought back. Over a hundred protesters were murdered by police snipers, and thirteen policemen were killed. By late February 2014, the armed protesters turned the tide, and Yanukovych fled Ukraine for Russia. These events are generally known as the Euromaidan and the Revolution of Dignity.

However, Putin called these events a 'fascist coup' and began an invasion of Ukraine. The Ukrainian army had been neglected and was more a source of corrupt enrichment for officers than a fighting force. Russia marched into Crimea unopposed and annexed it. In the course of the invasion most of Ukraine's navy deserted to the Russians. Crimea was low-hanging fruit. According to the 2001 census, two-thirds of its population was ethnically Russian and only a quarter Ukrainian. Over 80 per cent was Russophone. There were more Crimean-Tatar-speakers in Crimea than Ukrainian-speakers. The Crimean authorities had held referendums in the early 1990s to press for independence or at least expand their autonomy, but Kyiv quashed these efforts. After Russia took Crimea in 2014, it held its own referendum on 28 February. It was definitely a Soviet-style election, with 97 per cent of voters in favour of joining the Russian Federation.

At the same time, Russia encouraged anti-Maidan, pro-Russian unrest across the East and South of Ukraine, from Kharkiv in the northeast to Odesa in the southwest. Putin called this large swath of Ukraine 'Novorossiia,' a reference to a territorial unit carved out of the Crimean Khanate in 1764. The wave of pro-Russian protests, which often involved seizure of government buildings, was called 'the Russian Spring'. Owing to timely preventive measures by the hastily reconstituted Ukrainian government, the pro-Russian sepa-ratist movements only succeeded in the eastern Donbas region. Two cities – Donetsk and Luhansk – became the capitals of tiny separatist republics. But the battle over the eastern Donbas raged for another eight years, claiming about 15,000 lives. The two republics were first governed by rather thuggish military types, but later Russia installed leaders whom they controlled directly. Shelling from the Ukrainian side destroyed many buildings. The 'success' of the Russian Spring in the two republics discredited the separatist option among some who might have earlier been attracted to it.

After 2014 the Ukrainian government built up the country's armed forces, aided to some extent by Western countries, notably the USA and Canada. The president elected in the wake of the Euromaidan, Petro Poroshenko (2014–19), ran on a nationalist programme, appealing much more to the West of the country than to its East and South. He reinvigorated the cult of the OUN and UPA, appointing a Nationalist as head of the Ukrainian Institute of National Remembrance. He set quotas to assure that the Ukrainian language was dominant in TV and radio. This came at the expense of the Russian language, and naturally produced opposition from pro-Russian politicians. The Ukrainian language was also mandated as the exclusive language of education in state schools from the fifth grade on. This became a sore point in relations with Hungary, since there was a sizable Magyar-speaking minority in Transcarpathia.

Poroshenko also initiated a church reform that led to schism throughout the Eastern Orthodox world. Until early 2019, the Orthodox church in Ukraine was divided among three jurisdictions: the Ukrainian Orthodox Church, which was the largest religious organization in Ukraine and a self-governing church under the Patriarch of Moscow; the Ukrainian Orthodox Church (Kyivan Patriarchate), which was not recognized by any other Orthodox church; and the Ukrainian Autocephalous Church, also unrecognized and based primarily in Western Ukraine. Poroshenko, with some aid from the US State Department, was able to gain the support of the Patriarch of Constantinople to establish a united Ukrainian Orthodox church that would be under the jurisdiction of Constantinople rather than Moscow. In theory, there was to be a unification council of all three Orthodox churches in Ukraine, but in reality, and unsurprisingly, the Ukrainian Orthodox Church of the Moscow Patriarchate refused to participate. In the end, a rump unification council was held between the two formerly unrecognized Ukrainian churches, and a new church came into being, the Ukrainian Orthodox Church of Ukraine. It was an autocephalous church under the Patriarch of Constantinople. The Patriarch of Moscow condemned the new church and its patron in Constantinople, introducing a schism in world Orthodoxy.

Orthodox churches around the world had to make a choice whether to support Constantinople or Moscow. At least for the next few years (i.e., at the time this is being written), most Orthodox churches were unwilling to recognize the new Ukrainian church under Constantinople. Partially this reflected respect for the prestige and financial resources of the Russian church, and partially this resulted from resentment that Constantinople was interfering in the affairs of other churches. Parishes and communities in Ukraine were also divided. Poroshenko's government used various administrative measures to transfer parishes from the jurisdiction of the Moscow Patriarchate to the jurisdiction of the Orthodox Church of Ukraine. This was especially successful in the politically nationalist regions of Galicia and Volhynia. At present the Ukrainian Orthodox Church [Moscow Patriarch] claims over 12,000 parishes and the Orthodox Church of Ukraine claims over 7,000.

Poroshenko was aiming at the consolidation of the Ukrainian nation on an ethnonationalist platform, a Ukrainian nation that spoke Ukrainian, adopted a nationalist version of history, and worshipped in a Ukrainian church. This was also, and deliberately, an attempt to de-russify Ukraine. It is difficult to say whether his efforts over five years had a positive or negative impact on healing the regional divisions in Ukraine. What is not unclear is that his policies infuriated Putin.

Was Ukrainian society moving in the direction of ethnonationalism? The answer came in the 2019 presidential elections. Poroshenko ran for a second term as president. His slogan left no doubt that he intended to intensify his efforts: 'Army, Language, Faith'. Facing him was a celebrity candidate, a comedian named Volodymyr Zelenskiy. A rather diminutive figure, he had starred in a sitcom in which a teacher rants about the corruption in Ukraine, his rant goes viral, and he unexpectedly becomes president of Ukraine. And that's pretty much what happened in reality. For years, Ukrainian presidential candidates had been campaigning on symbols and historical memory politics and on pro-Russian and pro-Western platforms, while neglecting more concrete domestic issues and simultaneously enriching themselves. Zelenskiy ran on an anti-corruption programme, and he was able to overcome the regional political divisions that had plagued independent Ukraine since its inception. He received the largest percentage of the popular vote ever – 73 per cent. He won in every oblast of Ukraine except for the most recalcitrantly nationalist of them – Lviv oblast. Moreover, Zelenskiy was of Jewish rather than Ukrainian ethnicity and a Russophone.

Zelenskiy was president when Putin's Russia launched a massive invasion of Ukraine on 24 February 2022. His skills as an orator have served Ukraine well in the war, which – at the time of this writing – is still underway. At this point, Ukraine has been successful in keeping the Russian forces largely at bay, but certain cities – much of Mariupol, and parts of Kharkiv and Kyiv – have suffered the destruction of infrastructure and shortages of food, heat, medicine, and water as a result of Russian shelling. Many villages in the environs of these cities have endured even more acute devastation. Every day brings news of fresh atrocities. About a tenth of Ukraine's population has fled abroad, mainly to Poland.

Clearly, Ukraine is once again at a turning point. The fog of war is too thick at present to glimpse of what the ultimate meaning of this conflagration will be. The only thing for sure is that huge wounds are being inflicted on the country and its people, wounds that will take a very long time to heal.

'Ten Turning Points: A Brief History of Ukraine' was first published on 13 April 2022 by the Ukraine Solidarity Campaign, www.ukrainesolidaritycampaign.org/2022/ 04/13/ ten-turning-points-a-brief-history-of-ukraine

I'm a Ukrainian Socialist: Here's Why I Resist the Russian Invasion

Taras Bilous

As a socialist and internationalist, I abhor war. But the basic premise of self-determination justifies the resistance of ordinary Ukrainians to Vladimir Putin's brutal invasion of our country.

I'm writing from Ukraine, where I serve in the Territorial Defence Forces. A year ago, I couldn't have expected to be in this situation. Like millions of Ukrainians my life has been upturned by the chaos of war.

For the past four months, I have had the opportunity to meet people whom I would hardly have met under other circumstances. Some of them had never thought of taking up arms before February 24, but the Russian invasion forced them to drop everything and go to protect their families.

We often criticize the actions of the Ukrainian government and the way defence is organized. But they do not question the necessity of resistance and understand well why and for what we are fighting.

At the same time, during these months, I've tried to follow and participate in the discussions of the international left about the Russian-Ukrainian war. And the main thing that I now feel from these discussions is fatigue and disappointment. Too much time being forced to rebut obviously false Russian propaganda, too much time explaining why Moscow had no 'legitimate security concerns' to justify war, too much time asserting the basic premises of self-determination that any leftist should already agree with.

Perhaps most striking about many of these debates about the Russian-Ukrainian war is the ignoring of the opinion of Ukrainians. Ukrainians are still often presented in some left-wing discussions either as passive victims who should be sympathized with or as Nazis who should be condemned. But the far right makes up a clear minority of the Ukrainian resistance, while the absolute majority of Ukrainians support the resistance and do not want to be just passive victims.

Negotiations

Among even many well-intentioned people in recent months, there's been increasingly loud but ultimately vague calls for negotiations and a diplomatic settlement of the conflict. But what exactly does this mean? Negotiations between Ukraine and Russia took place for several months following the invasion, but they did not stop the war. Before that, negotiations on Donbas had lasted for more than seven years with French and German participation; but despite signed agreements and a cease-fire, the conflict was never resolved. On the other hand, in a war between two states, even the terms of surrender are usually settled at the negotiating table.

A call for diplomacy in itself means nothing if we don't address negotiating positions, concrete concessions, and the willingness of the parties to adhere to any signed agreement. All of this directly depends on the course of hostilities, which in turn depends on the extent of international military aid. And this can speed up the conclusion of a just peace.

The situation in the occupied territories of southern Ukraine indicates that Russian troops are trying to establish a permanent position there because they provide Russia with a land corridor to Crimea. The Kremlin uses the grain looted in these territories to support its client regimes and simultaneously threatens the whole world with famine by blocking Ukrainian ports. The agreement on unblocking the export of Ukrainian grain, signed on July 22 in Istanbul, was violated by Russia the day after it was signed by attacking the Odessa Sea Trade Port with missiles.

Meanwhile, high-ranking Russian politicians, such as the former president and current deputy chairman of the Security Council, Dmitry Medvedev, or the head of Roscosmos, Dmitry Rogozin, continue to write that Ukraine must be destroyed. There is no reason to believe that Russia will stop its territorial expansion, even if one day it becomes beneficial for the Kremlin to sign a temporary truce.

On the other hand, 80 per cent of Ukrainians consider territorial concessions unacceptable. For Ukrainians, giving up the occupied territories means betraying their fellow citizens and relatives, and putting up with the daily abductions and tortures perpetrated by occupiers. Under these conditions, the parliament will not ratify cession, even if the West forces the Ukrainian government to agree to territorial losses. This would only discredit President Volodymyr Zelenskiy and lead to the re-election of more nationalist authorities, while the far right would be rewarded with favourable conditions for recruiting new members.

Zelenskiy's government, of course, is neoliberal. Ukrainian leftists and trade unionists have organized extensively against his social and economic policies. However, in terms of war and nationalism, Zelenskiy is the most moderate politician who could have come to power in Ukraine after the 2014 annexation of Crimea and the start of the war in Donbas.

There's been some misunderstanding about his own record, too. For example, many authors now blame Zelenskiy for the nationalist language policy, centred around restrictions on the Russian language in the public sphere and including restriction of secondary education in the languages of national minorities. In fact, these language laws were adopted during the previous term of parliament. It is just that individual provisions of these laws came into force after Zelenskiy took office. His government has repeatedly tried to soften them, but each time backed down after nationalist protests.

Only a mass domestic movement for change in Russia can open the possibility for the restoration of stable relations between Ukraine and Russia in the future.

This was evident after the beginning of the invasion in Zelenskiy's frequent appeals to the Russians, his invitation to the Kremlin to negotiate, and his statements that the Ukrainian army would not try to retake the territories that were under Russian control before February 24 but would seek their return through diplomatic means in the future. If Zelenskiy were replaced by someone more nationalistic, the situation would become much worse.

I hardly need to spell out the consequences of that outcome. There would be even more authoritarianism in our domestic politics, revanchist sentiments would prevail, and the war would not stop. Any new government would be much less restrained from shelling Russian territory. With a reinvigorated far right, our country would be dragged ever deeper into a maelstrom of nationalism and reaction.

As someone who has seen the horrors of this war, I understand the desire for it to be over as soon as possible. Indeed, no one is more eager for the war to end than we who live in Ukraine, but it is also important to Ukrainians how exactly the war will end. At the beginning of the war, I too hoped that the Russian anti-war movement would force the Kremlin to end its invasion. But unfortunately, this didn't happen. Today, the Russian anti-war movement can only influence the situation by carrying out the small-scale sabotage of railways, military factories, and so on. Something bigger will be possible only after the military defeat of Russia.

Of course, under certain circumstances, it might be appropriate to agree to a ceasefire. But such a ceasefire would only be temporary. Any Russian success would strengthen Vladimir Putin's regime and its reactionary tendencies. It would not mean peace, but decades of instability, guerrilla resistance in the occupied territories, and recurrent clashes on the demarcation line. It would be a disaster not only for

Ukraine but also for Russia, where a reactionary political drift would intensify and the economy would suffer from sanctions, with severe consequences for ordinary civilians.

A military defeat of the Russian invasion is therefore also in the interests of the Russians. Only a mass domestic movement for change can open the possibility for the restoration of stable relations between Ukraine and Russia in the future. But if Putin's regime is victorious, that revolution will be impossible for a long time. Its defeat is necessary for the possibility of progressive changes in Ukraine, Russia, and the entire post-Soviet world.

What socialists should do

It's worth acknowledging that my focus has been largely on the domestic dimensions – for both Ukrainians and Russians – of the current conflict. For many leftists abroad, discussions tend to focus on its wider geopolitical implications. But in my opinion, in assessing the conflict, socialists should first of all pay attention to the people directly involved in it. And secondly, many leftists underestimate the threats posed by the possible success of Russia.

The decision to oppose the Russian occupation was not made by Joe Biden, nor by Zelenskiy, but by the Ukrainian people, who rose *en masse* in the first days of the invasion and lined up for weapons. Had Zelenskiy capitulated then, he would only have been discredited in the eyes of most of society, but the resistance would have continued in a different form, led by hard-line nationalist forces.

Besides, as Volodymyr Artiukh has noted in *Jacobin*, the West did not want this war. The United States did not want problems in Europe because it wanted to focus on the confrontation with China. Even less did Germany and France want this war. Although Washington has done a lot to undermine international law (we, like socialists anywhere in the world, will never forget the criminal invasion of Iraq, for instance), by supporting Ukrainian resistance to the invasion they are doing the right thing.

To put it in historical terms, the war in Ukraine is no more a proxy war than the Vietnam War was a proxy war between the United States on one side and the Soviet Union and China on the other. And yet, at the same time, it was also a national liberation war of the Vietnamese people against the United States as well as a civil war between supporters of North and South Vietnam. Almost every war is multi-layered; its nature can change during its course. But what does this give us in practical terms?

During the Cold War, internationalists did not need to laud the USSR to support the Vietnamese struggle against the United States. And it is unlikely that any socialists would have advised left-wing dissidents in the Soviet Union to oppose support for the Vietcong. Should Soviet military support for Vietnam have been resisted because the USSR criminally suppressed the Prague Spring of 1968? Why then, when it comes to Western support for Ukraine, are the murderous occupations of Afghanistan and Iraq considered serious counterarguments for aid?

Socialist internationalists must evaluate every conflict based on the interests of working people and their struggle for freedom and equality.

Instead of seeing the world as being composed solely of geopolitical camps, socialist internationalists must evaluate every conflict based on the interests of working people and their struggle for freedom and equality. The revolutionary Leon Trotsky once wrote that, hypothetically, if fascist Italy pursuing their interests had supported the anti-colonial uprising in Algeria against democratic France, the internationalists should have supported the Italian arming of the rebels. It sounds quite right, and this did not stop him from being an anti-fascist.

Vietnam's struggle did not just benefit Vietnam; the defeat of the United States there had a significant (if temporary) deterrent effect on American imperialism. The same is true with Ukraine. What will Russia do if Ukraine is defeated? What would prevent Putin from conquering Moldova or other post-Soviet states?

US hegemony has had terrible consequences for humanity and it's thankfully now in decline. However, an end of US supremacy can mean either a transition to a more democratic and just international order or a war of all against all. It can also mean a return to the policy of imperialist spheres of influence and the military redrawing borders, as in previous centuries.

The world will become even more unjust and dangerous if non-Western imperialist predators take advantage of American decline to normalize their aggressive policies. Ukraine and Syria are examples of what a 'multipolar world' will be like if the appetites of non-Western imperialisms are not reduced.

The longer this horrible conflict in Ukraine goes on, the more popular discontent in Western countries could grow as a result of the economic difficulties of the war and sanctions. Capital, which does not like the loss of profits and wants to return to 'business as usual', may try to exploit this situation. It can also be used by right-wing populists who do not mind sharing spheres of influence with Putin.

But for socialists to use this discontent to demand less aid to Ukraine and less pressure on Russia would be a rejection of solidarity with the oppressed.

'I'm a Ukrainian Socialist: Here's Why I Resist the Russian Invasion' was first published on 26 July 2022 by *Jacobin*, www.jacobin.com/2022/07/ukraine-russia-war-putin-socialism-resistance

'Not Exactly Surprising, But Awe-inspiring': Ukraine's Resistance

Interview with Yuliya Yurchenko

I'm originally from Vinnytsia [a medium-sized city some-what west of the middle of Ukraine], which is where I am now. I came back to Ukraine on the Ukraine Solidarity Campaign delegation in February, with a group of trade unionists, journalists and left-wing politicians. We had planned to visit different bits of Ukraine, but in the end stayed in Kyiv due to safety concerns – this was just before the start of the invasion, as it turned out. We wanted to meet Ukrainian politicians and representatives, but perhaps even more importantly civil society organizations, and in particular trade unionists and representatives of the left – the real left in practice, not just in name. In particular I wanted to meet comrades from Sotsialnyi Rukh and help gather and deliver their message to people in Britain and beyond. We wanted to hear these people's assessment of the situation, but also their aspirations for the kind of Ukraine they want to see in the longer term.

It must seem like a long time ago now?
It seems like forever, but also like it's been one long day... This is something a lot of people here have said about the last two months. As the war began, our delegation received a recommendation from the UK to leave Ukraine immediately. I stayed partly for personal reasons, because I wanted to be

with my family, but also because I wanted to be with my comrades. I think perhaps on a deeper level I felt stubborn and wanted to reject the situation where so many millions of Ukrainians over many decades have had to leave the country to seek better fortune elsewhere or because an external power tries to impose ideas about what its future should be, and threatens your very life.

I don't know how long I'll stay. There are meetings in Europe that Sotsialnyi Rukh want me to attend, including with MEPs [Members of the European Parliament], where we'll be laying out our economic programme, in particular the demands about debt cancellation and post-war reconstruction. It would make sense for me to go as I've been coordinating those campaigns.

Razem [the Polish left party], the Nordic left and some other sympathetic MEPs are helping us organize it. More broadly it's hard to know where you can be more useful, here or outside the country.

What do you think Putin's goals are? And what's your assessment of how the war's gone so far?
Well, there's a large element of speculation, but certain things are clear from the rhetoric that's come out of the Kremlin and its media mouthpieces. Moreover, that rhetoric goes back not just weeks but actually decades and there has been plenty of analysis of it.

We may not know Putin's exact plans for Ukraine, but we know that he and his supporters reject any notion of self-determination or even really autonomy for the country. They reject the idea that Ukraine is or can be a separate nation in its own right. Look at the article published by [Russian state news outlet] RIA Novosti [which argued essentially that Ukraine and 'Ukrainian-ness' as a whole must be suppressed]. The message is increasingly not even about liberating Donbas [in eastern Ukraine] from a 'junta' in Kiev. They're saying the whole country is corrupted by Nazism and needs 'denazifying'.

The reason Russian forces are mainly restricted to certain areas of the country is because they have suffered some military setbacks and the war has dragged on longer than they were planning.

I think they expected the West to do a deal and auction off Ukraine, which it would have done if the Ukrainian army and people hadn't fought tooth and nail.

Was this degree of resistance surprising to you?
Not exactly surprising but certainly awe-inspiring. I thought Ukrainians would resist and I thought much of the Russian leaders' calculation would be self-deluding, but the degree of both has perhaps surprised me.

I think Zelenskiy's instinct pre-invasion would have been to go for a deal with Russia to preserve civilian lives, perhaps partition of the country, and he is no doubt under pressure from the Western powers whose funding we are so dependent on. In the context of the great popular mobilization though, the territorial battalions, all the different volunteers, Ukrainian society as a whole, this is not such an easy option. Every time there are negotiations and rumours of a deal, you see a clear popular reaction, on social media and in communities. That popular pressure is surely an important factor in why the war has gone on longer than Russia predicted.

That in turn put pressure on Western governments to give us support and send us more, if still insufficient, weapons. All the recent atrocities, in Mariupol, in the areas around Kyiv, at Kramatorsk railway station, have reinforced that dynamic. We now see the German government, long the most defensive of Russia, seriously distancing themselves. This is very important, because Germany is such a central factor in Europe. Even Boris Johnson's attempts to save himself by turning into Churchill 2.0 have really weighed in favour of Ukraine. At the same time, it's not just the manoeuvring of governments – don't discount the stand taken by trade unions, by civil society, the demonstrations and mass pressure.

The situation is grim but more favourable than I would have imagined and I can even imagine a situation where Russia is forced out of Donbas.

Is it the case that people in the West see this as something that has just begun, whereas a lot of Ukrainians regard the war as starting eight years ago, when Russian forces entered eastern Ukraine, but now escalating?

In 2014 this was very much the case, but people have a great capacity to try to get on with their lives. Now, with this great escalation, that's not possible in the same way. What we should say is that already in 2014 Putin's attitude to Ukraine was very clear. We had a smaller scale Russian invasion eight years ago and all the while people in the so-called republics [in Donbas] were being kidnapped and tortured, the trade unions were being squashed, the Crimean Tatar people were being hounded out of the Crimean Peninsula. If people in Ukraine tried to get on with their lives to a certain degree, in the West these things were largely ignored. That would not have been the case if there was a war in the Netherlands, for example. Comrades from non-white, so to speak, countries have rightly pointed out how Ukrainians are now being treated differently, but in so far as this is true it was not previously the case and Ukrainians have long been the 'wrong kind of white' for the EU. Mind you, not all Ukrainians are white, of course.

Do you think that the reason solidarity with Ukraine and Ukrainians has entered people's consciousness so dramatically is because the governments and ruling classes of the West have taken it up, for their own reasons?

You have to distinguish who in society you're talking about, right? I think everyday people who are expressing solidarity are largely being absolutely genuine. There are plenty of organizations, labour movement and civil society organizations, that have expressed solidarity all the way through. There are those who have just taken these things up now, but they are still motivated by solidarity to various degrees. In the case of many politicians, however, I seriously doubt that is the case to the same extent. There were German politicians, for instance, who didn't want to help us even a few weeks ago and have now shifted for obviously self-interested reasons.

Those reasons include the fact that Putin is now also threatening other European states, the Baltic states and even Scandinavia. This is something that should concern us too. The threatening imperialist attitude way beyond Ukraine is quite open – [former Russian president Dimitry] Medvedev says they want 'Eurasia' to stretch from Vladivostok to Lisbon. Meanwhile Putin attacks Europe as 'Gayropa', and says that only the Russkii mir [Russian world] will save the planet from the culturally rotten West.

At the same time there are millions of refugees, who are not on boats in the Mediterranean, they are on the Polish border, and they cannot be pushed literally back into the sea, to certain death. This is another source of pressure on the Western states.

In terms of Donbas, from a socialist and democratic point of view, what kind of settlement should the left advocate?

There are clearly important social groups who want greater self-governance, and that is of course fine. You could have devolved autonomy within Ukraine, for instance similar to what used to exist in the Crimea. This needs to be debated and decided in a proper democratic way, without Russian troops, mercenaries and functionaries, and with proper international observation. All the people who have been forced to leave since 2014 must have the right to go back and take part in the process. At the same time there is a need for serious investment and economic cooperation to address the large-scale social and economic problems in the region, problems that have been horrendously exacerbated by the de-industrialization, de-development, and ecological degradation of the last eight years, which is not limited to Russia-controlled territories.

You have referred to Western military aid. How would you respond to Western leftists who say they're against Russia's war but don't want the West sending weapons to Ukraine?

By all means we can talk about pacifist solutions to conflicts before they begin. Now we're in a conflict that is a war of aggression, unprovoked, and where there are indiscriminate killings, torture and rape of civilians. I would also point out that Ukraine tried negotiations for eight years and the result was this invasion. If anybody from the UK Stop the War Coalition or some sort of hardcore pacifist organization wants to propose a practicable plan how to resolve this without fighting back, I would be genuinely interested. But I think the discussions proposed so far are frankly callous, delusional crap. Refusing weapons to Ukraine will not result in peace in any sense the left can or should support.

It will just mean Russia conquering the country more easily and being even less restrained in terrorising the population and repressing the very minorities it pretends to liberate; put briefly – if you appease the bully, they bully harder. If people want to argue that should happen in order to end the conflict and save lives, let them argue it openly and state which lives and towns they feel is fine to give up to Russia. I think it is both a losing and an immoral position.

It also seems like pretend pacifism?

Yes, indeed. There is an established tradition on the left of supporting armed resistance in African, Asian and Latin American countries against imperialist powers. But then in Ukraine you get objections about the Azov regiment – rightly so, but in reality, this kind of problem exists in almost all such conflicts.

At the root of it I think is seeing Russia as a counter-weight to the USA. They let their anti-Americanism and anti-NATOism get in the way of seeing the reality in Ukraine.

Tell us about Sotsialnyi Rukh and its work.

Sotsialnyi Rukh came together in 2015, a mix of established left-wing activists, involved in different political groupings and organizations, and young activists who were looking to create a meaningfully socialist organization in Ukraine, as opposed to one that just has 'socialist' or 'communist' in its name, as is the case in parts of Ukraine and other post-Soviet states. Those young comrades had been going on demonstrations and engaging in grassroots activism, but decided it was time to form a political organization – because protests and strikes will not by themselves overturn the oligarchic regime.

A big focus of work since then has been working with independent trade unions. The trade union movement in Ukraine has a divide between bureaucratic unions that came out of the Soviet era, and a new, independent union movement. There are new trade unions being organized in a range of sectors – in the health sector for instance, and in small and medium enterprises.

Sotsialnyi Rukh is active in helping to form and develop trade unions – for instance one of our comrades was involved in this in the construction sector, where he worked – and in helping organize demonstrations and strikes. We've been working with trade unions and workers to run a legal advice service for those whose rights are being violated. We also try to raise workers' consciousness, for instance through reading clubs and summer schools.

Since the war started we've been engaged in the volunteer movement, helping source medicine, food, clothes and protective gear for the territorial defence. By the way, there is also a left-wing battalion, organised by anarchists and socialists who are fighting in the territorial defence.

How did that come about?

You should speak to Taras Bilous about that, because he's part of it. Essentially, I think in the established battalions there is a risk of being associated with the wrong kind of people; and people therefore want to organize together with like-minded others. Many of those involved have known each other for a while, for instance through organizing protests outside illegal construction sites in defence of workers' rights.

But since February most of the stuff we've been doing is raising awareness about social problems caused by the war, deprivation, the problems facing internally displaced people, for instance the problems caused by profiteering in the housing market. In Lviv [in the far west of Ukraine] there are so many refugees that the housing market is completely screwed up – Aliona Liasheva wrote about it for *Spilne* [the left-wing *Commons* journal]. The work advising people on their labour rights is now even more important than before and there is also a major legal assault on workers' rights. Now we are also spearheading and coordinating the campaign for cancellation of Ukraine's foreign debt.

This is something that Sotsialnyi Rukh and its members have raised through different channels for some time, for instance through *Spilne*, which many comrades are involved in. There has been both academic-type analysis and campaigning already, but obviously the issue has become much more pressing.

In the war Ukraine's expenses have exploded because of humanitarian, medical and military needs, and meanwhile the preliminary assessment shows that we have already suffered losses amounting to a trillion US dollars! Even prior to the war Ukraine was the second largest debtor in terms of outstanding debt with the IMF, and it also has a lot of private debt. Now it is racking this up by issuing war bonds and so forth. We find it grotesque that the poorest country in Europe, fighting a war for the rest of Europe to contain

Russia, has to prioritize its debt repayments over meeting the exploding needs of its population. So we have ramped up campaigning, demanding that the debt is written off.

The Polish party Razem has been an amazing ally; they have been helping build an international network to lobby for our case.

Connected to this, there is a major question about assistance to Ukraine to rebuild after the war, which poses the question of what type of assistance. Obviously, part of that is reparations from Russia, funded by expropriating the assets of oligarchs. More broadly, people have talked about a new Marshall Plan, so we need to look what made the Marshall plan a success, and what were the positives and negatives in it. For instance, it included restrictions on left-wing political activity in the countries that received aid. So while demanding foreign aid we must defend political pluralism as sacrosanct, as an essential for the future of the country.

What is the Ukrainian government's attitude to debt cancellation?

They are very nervous about it, they don't like to hear about it, because what they hear is not cancellation but default, making it even more difficult for Ukraine to work with the international institutions and with investors in the future. The ministry of finance insists that Ukraine will honour its debts. They made a biannual payment on Eurobonds at the start of March, and there is another one due in September. They are trying to find creative ways to get round the problem of lack of funds, for instance issuing war bonds and finding ways to reorganize financial transfers with the IMF. They seem somewhat in denial about the fact that Ukraine simply does not have the necessary resources. So in our campaign we are trying to put pressure internationally, on the European Central Bank, on the US government, on the IMF – on Ukraine's major international 'partners'. If we can shift them then the Ukrainian government will of course accept it more easily.

Even in Britain it's quite hard to argue for socialism; it surely must be even harder in Ukraine where Stalinism has discredited the idea so much? Is that the case? Is it different with the younger generation?
I'm not the best person to speak to about this because I'm normally in the UK, but my observation is that a lot depends on the language. If you start with Lenin, you may well get a knee-jerk reaction. But if you start with people's position in society, and social inequality, and ask them what we should do about the oligarchs, you will get a better conversation. The same if you ask, Shouldn't the state provide decent pensions, healthcare, education and so on? And as a political economist I understand that the system that can provide those is very far from the unbridled market type.

Since 2014 in particular there has been a right-wing campaign around 'decommunization', linked to rejecting things connected to Russia and all things USSR. Obviously, this is absurd; you have to unpick the argument. What about the enterprises accumulated and built up during the USSR, which account for a huge chunk of the Ukrainian economy? Should they all be shut down? Should they be burnt down as an act of defiance? Second, who are people angry at? In 2014 the Soviet Union had been gone 25 years, and now over it's over 30. Who is responsible for the situation now? Then, if you talk to people about how the economy could be restructured and the need for decent social provision, you can get them on board, and you can explain that capitalism runs against these things.

These points make sense, but isn't what you're describing more social democracy than socialism?
Well, you can then raise further questions about who owns services and industries and how they are managed.

For instance, in terms of healthcare, OK, you can have a universal service, but who will pay for it and who will own it? Will it just be insurance for private hospitals? And actually, ironically, many people have a certain nostalgia for various kinds of public services that existed under the Soviet Union, for instance widespread local health facilities, which capitalism has since demolished. That can be tapped into. However, there is no doubt that these are more difficult conversations than in Britain, where there is a strong labour movement history that has not been interrupted in the same way.

It's been interrupted to a much less total extent, at least.

Yes. We're restarting in a way. The other thing that doesn't help us here is that we have parties that have 'socialist' in their names or in their propaganda but they have essentially been mechanisms for different fractions of the oligarchic class to carve up state property into their private property. There is a widespread hostility to the power of oligarchs, which was reflected in both the Euromaidan movement [in 2013–14] and then later in Zelenskiy's election, or rather how it was perceived. When people were in the squares for the Maidan, they were booing oligarchs who were trying to barter a deal with Yanukovych. It was in many respects a reactionary or reactive movement, there was a common thread of being pissed off at police brutality, lawlessness, corruption and the oligarchs remaining in power whoever was voted in. If Russia had not started the war in the east [in 2014], it is conceivable we would have seen more of a social or class-struggle movement developing by now.

We had [Petro] Poroshenko [Ukrainian president 2014–19], whose pitch was that he was the best commander-in-chief for the war, and then he was rejected in favour of the populist Zelenskiy. It was a kind of Maidan protest in the voting booths, though in reality Zelenskiy is not anti-oligarch. There is a crisis of representation that the left could tap into, though how soon a substantial political force will emerge I don't know. Not necessarily the next election, but maybe not so long after that.

For now Zelenskiy presumably remains very popular?
Yes, because he's a very effective performer, and also because he has proven himself as a war-time leader. I imagine if we have a free election he will be re-elected. But the composition of the cabinet and certainly the parliament, how oligarchic-dominated it is and what kind of laws it makes, will be very important. There will the neo-liberal puppets of the appropriators [capitalists] who say the solution for post-war reconstruction is to liberalize everything even further, which will damage reconstruction as well as increasing inequality.

What are trade unions doing during the war? Are they still functioning in workplaces?
Of course there is a large degree of disruption. It depends which unions we're talking about, what industries, how close they are to where the fighting is happening. But yes, they are still functioning and doing some important work. I think there were some lessons learnt after 2014 about how to keep contact with their members in the [Russian] occupied territories. One of the most impressive examples is the work done by Ukrainian railway workers and their unions, who throughout all this have worked to evacuate people and bring in supplies, even in areas where there is shelling and the tracks have been bombed.

There is also a dialogue with the government about workers' rights, which is very necessary because as you know there has been a suspension of some workers' rights. I believe that resulted in some elements of this change being rolled back, but I will check that for you [The Rada passed a law reducing workers' rights in July 2022].

Can you say something about the strength of the far right in Ukraine? Obviously, this is widely discussed, or rather raised but not really discussed, on the Western left.

The far right is a problem. Since it was founded, Sotsialnyi Rukh has had conflict with these right-wing groups and in some cases our members have been physically attacked. There are websites where they create lists of *levaki*, 'lefties', for their people to target. Then they have wider activities like harassing gay rights parades or women's day parades and trying to start fights there. And they have a relationship with the police, who regard these groups as doing a useful job for them. A cop may lose their job if they beat up a protester, so they can let the fascist do it for them. Even when they carry out arrests of the far right it does not usually lead to any serious consequences. Of course such a situation exists in many countries. It doesn't necessarily mean that these groups have widespread social support.

In terms of the war and the army, you know about Azov. They were significantly more radical before 2014, and since then they have mellowed a bit, though of course they are still very vicious nationalists and some are actual Nazis. But now it seems some join them because of right-wing ideology and some because the regiment is famous and well organized and of course is part of the army itself. On one hand that makes them subject to all kinds of restrictions and controls on their activities, but on the other it is a serious problem in itself.

It is not clear how much the war has boosted them. Certainly, in the siege of Mariupol they have appeared to many as heroic defenders. I'm not convinced it will lead to wider support, because unlike in 2014 they are submerged in a much wider mobilization of Ukrainians as a broader political category. A bigger problem is broader hostility to Russians, which of course is understandable but totally wrong, rather than the far right specifically.

Thanks so much for taking this time. Last question, how does this war and the situation in Ukraine fit into the wider picture of 21st-century capitalism, and how socialists should respond to it?

Even though this is a just war on Ukraine's side, there is a real risk it will cement neoliberalism and militarization further. We already see countries ramping up their military spending.

On a range of issues, from the rights of refugees to the question of international debt, the left needs to use this opportunity to draw out wider lessons, to talk about deprived nations whose rights have been overlooked in recent years, and to make arguments about the inadequacy of international institutions that at best have done nothing to prevent all the horrors of war, indebtedness and social destruction. These institutions have brought disaster to what 'naturally' should be some of the richest countries in the world, in Africa and Latin America for instance.

So, there is a lot to grab hold of here. For instance, with the debt campaign, we are linking up with the International Committee for the Abolition of Illegitimate Debt, the Debt Jubilee Campaign and other groups to revive a dialogue about what should happen if a country finds itself in a state of war or natural disaster, about the idea of an automatic mechanism for suspending debt payments and replacing them with aid. This will not bring a revolution but it could be important for winning more ground.

I think we should argue for the UN to be democratized, and as part of that for the permanent section of the Security Council to be disbanded. The aim should be an international security architecture which at least sets the goal of every country being protected, no matter who or where they are.

Leaders and activists in Africa, for instance, are frustrated about Ukraine getting more attention or more consideration than other countries facing emergencies and what this says about international institutional racism. The answer is not competition over who gets a little bit more of the pie, but working together on the basis of recognizing that many countries are being fucked by international capitalism. It's one country today, tomorrow it will be another – we need to argue and fight to sort out the systemic problems. I think there could be a bit more space for international solidarity opening up, and the demand for debt cancellation could be one mechanism for that.

We have to do all this while challenging the ramping up of neoliberalism on one hand, and on the other hand animosity towards Russia and Russians as such when the war is over. We need to argue for international reconciliation and a restructuring of the global economy and institutions.

This interview was conducted by Sasha Ismail and Michael Baker and first published on 4 May 2022, www.workersliberty.org/story/2022-05-04/not-exactly-surprising-awe-inspiring-yuliya-yurchenko-ukraines-resistance

Ten Terrible Leftist Arguments Against Ukrainian Resistance

Oksana Dutchak

Discussions with some on the (mostly) Western left can be extremely hard. Some of their positions are disheartening to hear. Others seem hypocritical or cynical. There are, in my opinion, certain positions that are far from left principles. These points are not always expressed directly, so I want to briefly dig into some hidden messages underlying positions held by many on the left.

Disclaimer #1: I want to stress that there are also a lot of leftists who take the position of solidarity and will have zero to do with these claims. However, here I am not writing about them.

Disclaimer #2: It really matters how some of these messages are voiced as this draws the line between, on the one hand, points of concern and discussion, and on the other – the central pillar of one's predetermined and uncon- ditional political stand against Ukrainian resistance. This text is about the second case. I won't discuss nuances here. This is a polemic opinion piece, not an analytical article.

Disclaimer #3: I'm frustrated, angry and, hence, often sarcastic here. And yes, I have the right to be so. And yes, I use this piece to channel my frustration and anger.

***

1
'If another country attacked my country, I would just flee'

Well, I've done the same because I have two children. The unvoiced full version of the claim: *'In a hypothetical situation, which is highly unlikely, but which I still project on you, I will not support any collective resistance to the invasion and because of this projection I oppose Ukrainian resistance'.* This claim is mostly expressed by people from countries without any modern history of being subject to nor under the threat of imperial domination. But we are not in an abstract war here or in any version of your projections. It is a very concrete imperial invasion backed by the rhetoric of total submission. Sometimes it also reaches the level of genocidal rhetoric. A Marxist should have a triple facepalm hearing that the war against imperial oppression is not worth fighting. Of course, if something like this ever happens to you, you can choose the option of not resisting and I would never judge you as long as you don't use your individual choice to condemn the collective defensive struggle of others in a totally and structurally different reality.

2
'I would never fight for my government'

The unvoiced full version of the claim: *'1) Ukrainians are fighting for their government, 2) I think so for no reason and I either have not checked this claim with Ukrainians or 3) I don't think Ukrainians' opinion should be taken into account anyway.'* Well, quite obvious – this war has nothing to do with our shitty (like many others) government. Check the fucking opinion polls which some leftists like so much when they support their point and immediately forget about when they undermine it. If this war ever had anything to do with the Ukrainian government, the government stopped being relevant the second Russian propaganda started to talk about 'the solution of the Ukrainian question' and 'denazification' of the population, *en masse.*

The second part of this unvoiced claim is tied to a total detachment from material reality and disregard of it – a very materialist approach, indeed. The third part of the claim has, of course, nothing to do with left principles and is, unfortunately, like many other points, an obvious manifestation of West-centric, patronizing or arrogant 'leftism'.

Probably the most stunning variations of this position are 'analyses' of the war with numerous factual mistakes by people who know almost nothing about the region, and manifestos 'against the war' without a single Ukrainian signature. Being a left academic 'superstar' is a guarantee many people will still take your text seriously, despite the desperately lamenting material reality and human bodies buried under its rubble.

3
'Our government supports Ukraine and I can never take the side of my government'

The unvoiced full message of this claim is: *In fact I do support my government in many instances, but in such a way I justify my stand against supporting Ukrainian resistance and / or rely on identity politics instead of materialist principles to make my life conformist and simple.'* Of course, these people support their governments on some occasions and criticize and oppose it on others. Reality is complicated, you know. Sometimes even shitty governments do the right thing, especially under pressure from popular progressive struggle. It is like opposing migrants and refugees, which the government decided to 'let in', because it was the government's position. (I know, I know that some do this under the slogan that 'they will take our workers' jobs'.) An illusory principled opposition to one's own government is simply used, again, as a justification of opposition to Ukrainian resistance. Seriously supporting this claim means relying on identity politics based on blind universalization instead of an analysis of the material reality facing Ukraine.

4
'Ukrainian and Russian workers, instead of fighting with each other, should turn their guns against their own governments'

The unvoiced message here is: *'I prefer to do nothing in this situation where there is no direct or indirect threat to my life, I'm opposing Ukrainian resistance and I want to find a nice, leftist-sounding justification.'* Yeah, we should better pretend to be stones and wait for a global proletarian revolution. Well, I'm afraid at some moment such people will even claim there is no need to wage any social struggle until the global revolution (I know, I know that some almost do). This position, however, is (often) the position of a privileged individual which hides ideological egoism behind nice rhetoric. It is also a product of the years-long decline in left mobilization and the global system's many reactionary turns. A very good and universal shit, if somebody wants to do the shitbath, I recommend this one.

5
'Who benefits from this war?'

The unvoiced message is: *'I know that some parts of the elite capitalist class benefit almost from anything in this world, because it is how the system works, but I still use this question (which is not really a question) to express my opposition to Ukrainian struggle for self-determination.'* Opposing such a struggle because Western elites benefit from it is like opposing industrial action because a capitalist competitor benefits from it. Another variation of this claim is part of the NATO weapon discussion (though, of course, I know the discussion is more complicated). Sorry, but we live in a world without a progressive state of the size required to provide material support to a struggle of this scale and benefit from its victory. Unless you consider other imperial powers like China to be progressive.

This shithole is also a good one to go for as it is a deep one and can contain many variations. Most of the discussion about the 'spheres of influence' falls into this shithole too in one way or another. Taking this position seriously means taking the side of the reactionary status quo we have been living in for decades. It also often goes together with denial, devaluation or even favouritism of Russian (or any non-Western) imperialism. Sometimes it also hides all the other thoughts, like supporting any cannibalistic regime against Western imperialism. On the part of some leftists from the Global South it can hide the lust for revenge – this lust, though being far more understandable than the conformist identity politics of Western observers, contains a nasty disregard of Ukrainian people at whose expense the revenge against Western imperialism must be waged.

6
'What about the far right on the Ukrainian side?'

The hidden claim here is: *'I use the far-right problem as a fig leaf to hide my opposition to Ukrainian resistance.'* Yeah, there are far right groups in Ukraine – like in many other countries – and yes, they have weapons now because, surprise, we are at war. But those who voice this claim mostly don't care about the far right on the side of the Russian army or the general scary far-right path of Russian politics with respective implications for its internal and foreign 'affairs' (like, yeah, the row of wars). They don't care that some left political scientists from Russia now call their regime a post-fascist one. They don't know about how big is the participation of far right in Ukrainian resistance, they don't care about participation of other ideological groups and the general scale of the resistance, they don't know how the empty signifier of 'Nazi' is used by Russian propaganda to dehumanize whoever they want. It is just a fig leaf which, thanks to Russian propaganda and some other factors, has grown into a colossus.

7
'Russia and Ukraine should negotiate.
Upgraded version: here are our
propositions for a peace deal'

This claim has many hidden variations, which depend on the propositions of the peace deal those people voice. Depending on these propositions, the unvoiced message can be: *1) Ukraine should capitulate or 2) we are detached from reality and think our relatively reasonable propositions of a peace deal are realistic now.* The first option is the same good old 'peace by any means': the propositions basically presuppose that Ukraine should give up on newly captured territories and follow almost all the absurd political demands of Russia, giving up the country's independence and people's self-determination. Very leftist, indeed. In the second option the proposed peace deal is close to the one that was on the negotiation table in spring, when the full-scale invasion started. One of the main points of the proposed peace deal is that the Russian army must retreat from the newly captured territories – to the border on the 23rd of February. This point makes the whole proposition useless at this moment of time and the proposers cannot give a reasonable answer to the questions why should the Putin regime do that at this stage, and how and by who can it be 'persuaded' to do this.

There is also the uglier version of the unvoiced message: *'We are sane, knowing our relatively reasonable propositions are unrealistic at the moment, but we still voice them to show that those stupid Ukrainians don't want to negotiate.'*

8
'The West should stop supporting Ukraine
because it may escalate into a nuclear war'

The hidden message: *'Any nuclear country can do whatever it wants because we are afraid.'* You know, I'm also afraid of nuclear war. But keeping to this position is supporting the reactionary status quo and facilitating imperialist politics. And what is missing from this discussion are the disastrous consequences of Russia's attack for the global movement for nuclear disarmament. Now I can hardly imagine why any country would give up its nuclear arsenal voluntarily being afraid to follow the 'destiny' of Ukraine (google 'Budapest Memorandum'). And this is not the West to blame here.

9
'We won't even talk to you because you are for weapons'

The hidden message: *'We don't care about the material reality of this war and sorry-not-sorry that you were unlucky enough to be attacked by a non-western imperial country, just do not make uncomfortable interventions into our imagined monolithic unipolar and west-centric internationalism.'* This is, of course, an intersection of many of the previous claims but I've decided to put it separately because this is a brilliant manifestation we, Ukrainian leftists, hear sometimes and wonder about solidarity, internationalism, attention to the structures of power inequality, anti-imperialism and all that, you know, important things, thrown into the trash in broad daylight in front of our eyes.

10
'Good Russian resistance vs. bad/inconvenient/ non-existing Ukrainian resistance'

And last, but not least – actually this one triggers me the most. This shit triggers me immensely and brings some irrational emotions I'm ashamed of. There is no hidden message here. One of the extreme examples is when the left meeting is addressed by a Russian anti-war activist and everybody listens, but when the same meeting is addressed by a Ukrainian left with basically the same messages, some people demonstratively leave the room and boo. The Ukrainian leftists can be questioned as if they have no right to participate in a discussion about this war if no Russian war-opposer is involved – even if just in a few days they participate in another discussion with Russian anti-war representatives. How dare the Ukrainian leftists speak about Russian invasion without the Russian leftists, right?

These are only extreme examples, but there is a sea of moderate variations: supporting and admiring Russian anti-war resistance and being numb to the Ukrainian one. Spreading some messages of the Russian anti-war movement and ignoring the messages of Ukrainian leftists. Pretending Ukrainian resistance does not exist. Writing about brave and strong Russian war-opposers and, at the same time, describing Ukrainians only as civilian losses, refugees, poor victims.

Russian anti-war resistance often voices similar claims and supports the Ukrainian left in relation to the war: they demand weapons for Ukrainian resistance, they want Russia to lose! Puzzling, that this similarity doesn't matter, right? However, the explanation is simple. Russian anti-war resistance is comfortable, it corresponds to many hidden claims and messages. They are against their government. They don't have guns in their hands. In the end, they are brave and worth listening to, unlike poor / stubborn / national-istic / militaristic – in other words, inconvenient – Ukrainian left, who refuse to be comfortable victims. You know why this difference between Ukrainian left resistance and Russian anti-war resistance appeared? Because it is not Russia which is under imperial attack, and it is not the Russian opposition which is waging a defensive war for self-determination.

***

I know some hidden claims and messages are missing. Some of them are so obviously bullshit to discuss, like 'But the USA has done much worse', 'socialist Russia', 'Nazi regime in Kiev', '14,000 civilians, killed by Ukrainian government', 'Don't be so emotional', 'There is nothing good to defend in Ukraine' (yes, this is a real one!). There are also some points which are too painful for me to discuss now.

I know that internationalism and practical solidarity are not falling apart for the first time. But you cannot even approach (again) its reconstruction, ignoring what is behind the hidden messages: idealistic delusions, structures of political power inequality, reactionary currents and all the other shit which allows so many to look away in the face of Russian imperialism and Ukrainian struggle for self-determination.

'Ten Terrible Leftist Arguments against Ukrainian Resistance' was first published on 20 July 2022 by *Commons*, an online left-wing journal of social criticism in Ukraine, at www.commons.com.ua/en/10-zhahlivih-livackih-argumentiv-proti-ukrayinskogo-oporu

'The Right to Resist':
A Feminist Manifesto

We, feminists from Ukraine, call on feminists around the world to stand in solidarity with the resistance movement of the Ukrainian people against the predatory, imperialist war unleashed by the Russian Federation. War narratives often portray women as victims. However, in reality, women also play a key role in resistance movements, both at the frontline and on the home front: from Algeria to Vietnam, from Syria to Palestine, from Kurdistan to Ukraine.

The authors of the Feminist Resistance Against War manifesto deny Ukrainian women this right to resistance, which constitutes a basic act of self-defence of the oppressed. In contrast, we view feminist solidarity as a political practice which must listen to the voices of those directly affected by imperialist aggression. Feminist solidarity must defend women's right to independently determine their needs, political goals, and strategies for achieving them. Ukrainian feminists were struggling against systemic discrimination, patriarchy, racism, and capitalist exploitation long before the present moment. We conducted and will continue to conduct this struggle both during war and in peacetime. However, the Russian invasion is forcing us to focus on the general defence effort of Ukrainian society: the fight for survival, for basic rights and freedoms, for political self-determination. We call for an informed assessment of a specific situation instead of abstract geopolitical analysis which ignores the historical, social and political context. Abstract pacifism which condemns all sides taking part in the war leads to irresponsible solutions in practice. We insist on the essential difference between violence as a means of oppression and as a legitimate means of self-defence.

The Russian aggression undermines the achievements of Ukrainian feminists in the struggle against political and social oppression. In the occupied territories, the Russian army uses mass rape and other forms of gender-based violence as a military strategy. The establishment of the Russian regime in these territories poses the threat of criminalizing LGBTIQ+ people and decriminalizing domestic violence. Throughout Ukraine, the problem of domestic violence is becoming more acute. Vast destruction of civilian infrastructure, threats to the environment, inflation, shortages, and population displacement endanger social reproduction. The war intensifies gendered division of labour, further shifting the work of social reproduction – in especially difficult and precarious conditions – onto women. Rising unemployment and the neoliberal government's attack on labour rights continue to exacerbate social problems. Fleeing from the war, many women are forced to leave the country, and find themselves in a vulnerable position due to barriers to housing, social infrastructure, stable income, and medical services (including contraception and abortion). They are also at risk of getting trapped into sex trafficking.

We call on feminists from around the world to support our struggle. We demand:

- The right to self-determination, protection of life and fundamental freedoms, and the right to self-defence (including armed) for the Ukrainian people – as well as for other peoples facing imperialist aggression.
- A just peace, based on the self-determination of the Ukrainian people, both in the territories controlled by Ukraine and its temporarily occupied territories, in which the interests of workers, women, LGBTIQ+ people, ethnic minorities and other oppressed and discriminated groups will be taken into account.

- International justice for war crimes and crimes against humanity during the imperialist wars of the Russian Federation and other countries.
- Effective security guarantees for Ukraine and effective mechanisms to prevent further wars, aggression, escalation of conflicts in the region and in the world.
- Freedom of movement, protection and social security for all refugees and internally displaced persons irrespective of origin.
- Protection and expansion of labour rights, opposition to exploitation and super exploitation, and democratization of industrial relations.
- Prioritization of the sphere of social reproduction (kindergartens, schools, medical institutions, social support, etc.) in the reconstruction of Ukraine after the war.
- Cancellation of Ukraine's foreign debt (and that of other countries of the global periphery) for post-war reconstruction and prevention of further austerity policies.
- Protection against gender-based violence and guaranteed effective implementation of the Istanbul Convention.
- Respect for the rights and empowerment of LGBTIQ+ people, national minorities, people with disabilities and other discriminated groups.
- Implementation of the reproductive rights of girls and women, including the universal rights to sex education, medical services, medicine, contraception, and abortion.
- Guaranteed visibility for and recognition of women's active role in the anti–imperialist struggle.
- Inclusion of women in all social processes and decision-making, both during war and in peacetime, on equal terms with men.

Today, Russian imperialism threatens the existence of Ukrainian society and affects the entire world. Our common fight against it requires shared principles and global support. We call for feminist solidarity and action to protect human lives as well as rights, social justice, freedom, and security.

We stand for the right to resist. If Ukrainian society lays down its arms, there will be no Ukrainian society. If Russia lays down its arms, the war will end.

Individual signatures

Including: Victoria Pigul, feminist, activist of 'Social Movement'; Oksana Dutchak, feminist, co-editor of *Commons: Journal of Social Criticism*; Oksana Potapova, feminist activist, researcher; Anna Khvyl, feminist, composer, curator; Daria Saburova, researcher, member of the 'European Network of Solidarity with Ukraine'; Hanna Manoilenko, activist at FemSolution collective; Hanna Perekhoda, member of the 'European Network of Solidarity with Ukraine'; Iryna Yuzyk, human rights activist, journalist.

The full list of Ukrainian individual signatories can be viewed at www.commons.com. ua/en/right-resist-feminist-manifesto

Organisations

Feministychna Maisternia / Feminist Workshop (feminist organization); Rebel Queers (feminist organization); Feministychna Loga / Feminist lodge (grassroots feminist organization currently providing vulnerable women and their families with humanitarian aid); Sfera / Sphere (organization representing the LGBT+ community and the women of Eastern Ukraine); Insha / Different (LGBTQI+ feminist and inclusive organization from city of Kherson); FemSolution (grassroots feminist initiative); Insait / Insight (LGBTQI+ organization); Centre for Social and Gender Studies 'New Life' (human rights organization specialized in gender mainstreaming and struggle against gender based violence); Development of Democracy Centre (human rights organization); Khlib Nasushnyi / Daily Bread (horizontal freeganic cooperative, engaging in food activism); QueerLab (cooperative that provides workplaces and / or necessary services and products to refugees); Institute of Gender Programs (organization promoting human rights and gender equality in the defence sector in the context of Russian aggression); D.O.M.48.24 (women's rights, development of social entrepreneurship, development of culture); Sotsialnyi Rukh / Social Movement (left organization that stands on the principles of people's power, anticapitalism, antixenophobia); Politychna Diya Zhinok / Political action of women (defending women's political rights); Ekolohichna Platforma / Ecological platform (eco-anarchist); NGO 'Centre of Gender Culture' (gender education).

'The Right to Resist' was first published on 7 July 2022 by *Commons*, at www.commons. com.ua/en/right-resist-feminist-manifesto

Our Main Goal Now Is to Win This War

Interview with Viktoriia Pihul

The Russian invasion of Ukraine is having an appalling impact on women and girls, especially among marginalized populations like the Roma. In bare summary:

- Military strikes have targeted maternity hospitals and other healthcare facilities, killing and wounding women and children, including pregnant women and new-born babies.
- Rape is used as a weapon of war.
- Access to essential health services is practically non-existent in those parts of Ukraine that are under severe attack, as well as being badly hit in the rest of the country.
- Gender-based violence, including sexual violence is increasing, increasing the risks of exploitation, including sexual exploitation and trafficking.
- Millions of women and girls are internally displaced or refugees.

In this interview of Viktoriia Pihul by Dick Nichols of Green Left, the Ukrainian feminist, anti-capitalist activist in Sotsialnyi Rukh (Social Movement) and initiator with other feminists of the manifesto 'The Right to Resist' explains how Ukraine's women are organizing and fighting back in the appalling conditions created by Putin's war. Emphases in the text are by Viktoriia Pihul.

How is the feminist movement trying to best cope and help with the present disaster? What are its priorities?

The war we now live through has affected and changed every aspect of our lives. The occupiers are working, among other things, to demoralize the population. That is why they use all means, including violence. At this very moment we need to understand that rape is a way of showing power and control over a situation, not a desire for sexual contact.

Of course, the work of feminist organizations under these conditions has changed considerably. Before the war, feminists and those who fought with us for women's rights and visibility did a very large part of the educational work: educational courses, programmes and events; organizing actions, marches, etc.

Now this work is being transformed and assistance is primarily focused on survival and humanitarian support: finding humanitarian aid, medicines for trans representatives, creating shelters, helping women with children to find or provide babysitting services. Social Movement, for example, collects humanitarian aid for women and children from trade unions. Organizations with which we have friendly relations, like Femsolution, Feminist Lodge and Bilkis, now do likewise.

This is a contradictory moment: on the one hand, the feminist movement is getting closer to women, hearing their voices. *The good point for women's rights is that women lead and are more engaged in community humanitarian efforts.* It provides opportunities for humanitarian actors to seek women's participation and guidance. I think that it is very important to focus on this: *women are involved in very important processes that allow Ukrainians to live and survive in the rear-guard.*

On the other hand, many of the problems that the movement has worked on for years risk becoming 'not now' issues. And what women are now doing to help win may be overlooked in public discourse. Because all attention is now focused on military operations and men's role, and the female contribution at the front will be less noticeable as well. That is, the inequality in the representation of female and male roles does not disappear during the war, but rather increases.

I see potential spaces for feminist work as grassroots activism and work with women to build cohesion, awareness of our visibility, and further struggle for women's political participation. For example, gender quotas, the work of gender commissioners, the promotion and implementation of the Istanbul Convention, which was ratified last month in Ukraine, working with the problem of domestic violence, the creation of shelters for women. *All this can be realized when women want to represent their interests and fight the stereotype that in politics everything is done by a few great people, and they do not decide anything.*

> **Olena Zelenskaya [Ukraine's 'First Lady'] has said: 'Our resistance, as our future victory, has taken on a particularly feminine face. Women are fighting in the army, they are signed up to territorial defence [units], they are the foundation of a powerful volunteer movement to supply, deliver, feed … they give birth in shelters, save their children, and look after others' children, they keep the economy going, they go abroad to seek help. Others are simply doing their jobs, in hospitals, pharmacies, shops, transport, public services … so that life continues.' How accurate is this picture of women's engagement in the fight against the Russian invasion?**

In this context I want to underline that gender roles are now changing in Ukraine. *Women on the home front have a war going on, too, which is just as important.*

Zelenskaya's words really reflect what I have seen in these more than four months of war.

With many people becoming unemployed and primarily men joining the Armed Forces of Ukraine, women are taking on new roles and multiple jobs to make up for the lost family income. Many women, forced to leave their homes and possessions behind, find themselves needing to buy household necessities all over again in a new place. By the way, the state has provided one-time assistance of 6500 *hryvnia* (€220) to Ukrainians, but this is very little taking inflation into account.

At the same time, women are now spending more and more time with children, as they are on distance education. Women very often decide to stay in the occupied territories to care for elderly parents or others. Or they are afraid of losing their sources of income. Thus, they are increasingly at risk of violence, both from the Russians and domestic psychological abuse.

All this creates an additional burden and requires a lot of effort on the part of women. *I want to emphasize that they often take their work and their contribution to the resistance for granted.* It is our task as feminists to support women, to recognize their needs and to help in any way we can. The most important thing is not to let the female face of war remain in the shadows.

How important for the overall morale of the resistance against the Russian invasion has the big increase in women's participation in the army and volunteer organizations been?

From the very first, we were all on adrenaline, taking on all kinds of things: volunteering, searching for ammunition, humanitarian aid, transporting people out of dangerous areas. With time, of course, this phase is replaced by immersion in trauma and helplessness.

But I hear and see in the public space women saying, *'We have no right to give up.'* As I said, women have begun to band together locally to help. They weave camouflage nets, cook food for the military, pack and ship humanitarian aid. This promotes cohesion, so women feel they are not alone in their grief. It seems to me that even psychologically there is a certain support in this that we hold on to. *Now voluntary work has become not something from the world of activists, but something close and understandable to almost everyone.*

As for women's participation in the army, I immediately remember our Пташка (that's 'bird' in Ukrainian) from Azovstal. This girl Katya, who defended Azovstal in Mariupol until her last day. She sang songs and said she would fight to the last. Her photo and video of her singing went viral on all social networks. She became one of the symbols of the defence of Mariupol.

Now 35,000 women serve in the Ukrainian military, 1000 of them are commanders, and two are generals. It is important that women also went from the first day of the war into territorial defence. Now there is more talk about women's participation in the army, and they are becoming an example for all of us who are on the home front.

Regarding attitudes in the Ukrainian Army, Hromadske International noted in 2014: 'To be honest there's nothing to celebrate yet as the changes are very slow. In the General Staff of Ukraine's Armed Forces you can hear the phrase 'my dear', so the army needs to be reformed starting with them. Many don't understand that significant changes will only take place after more than one generation.' That comment would seem to be confirmed by the army celebration of the 30th anniversary of Ukrainian Independence, which saw women soldiers marching in high heels. Is the seriousness of the resistance struggle against the Russian invasion helping put an end to this sort of sexist nonsense?

Sexism and inequality are still present in the army. In 2014, women who were, for example, snipers or artillerymen, were written in the employment record book as 'communications officer' or something similar, and they received less money. In eight years, the situation has changed, but globally the problems remain. *For example, at the beginning of the full-scale war women were issued with men's flak jackets and shoes, which are often larger in size, because there were no small ones. Women's body armour is also very different, but there was none.* So too with hygiene items: pads, shampoos, mosquito repellent and even hairpins. I want to mention the volunteer initiative Zemliachky: they are very supportive of women who serve and do humanitarian aid for women who are fighting, given their special needs.

As to public stereotyping, I want to share one case that impressed not only the feminist movement, but also most people who do not belong to it. A Ukrainian stand-up comedian at the end of May (when it was three months into the war) 'joked' as follows: 'Can you imagine what a women's battalion would look like? I can't. Would it be a battalion of sucking troops' … and further references to blowjobs. It was a blatant case of devaluation, sexism and toxic masculinity. What's more, people in the audience laughed, and a stand-up YouTube channel posted the video on their page (and still hasn't deleted it). This video was sent to one of the feminists by a woman who had fought in Debaltsevo in 2015 and had seen hell on earth, including the torn bodies of her comrades. One can only imagine how she felt when she saw this video.

Also, one musician, who joined the military forces of Ukraine, on March 8 in his Instagram 'congratulated' those guys who are hiding from the army, with the inference that they are supposedly women. These are just examples of recent high-profile cases, but on a domestic level there is still an unequal perception of women and men who are fighting. *But those men who are in the Armed Forces with women note their courage, fearlessness and bravery.* Various volunteer initiatives make social films and projects to bring women in the army out of the shadows and show how they are on a par with men in combat, and the men themselves attest to this. *I think that this war will break down a lot of stereotypes. But still, it is a very high price to pay.*

In times of crisis – of defence of invaded nations and civil wars – women fighters always appear, for example, on the Republican side in the Spanish Civil War, the Soviet women in the Great Patriotic War and more recently the women battalions in Rojava, so important in the defeat of Islamic State. What similarities and differences with these experiences do you see in the engagement of Ukrainian women in the resistance to the Russian invasion?

I think that Ukraine now has its own character.

It is very different from the Soviet narrative of 'War Has No Woman's Face' and it is not like the resistance of women in Rojava, because Kurdish women had to fight for basic rights and representation in society. In Spain there were constant conflicts about how women tried to fight for the right to fight as equals in the Republican army, but they were constantly thrown into secondary roles. It is difficult for me to say anything about the position of women in the army now, as that is best said by the women themselves after some time in the war has passed.

From what we can see, women's position in the army is surprisingly good, but surrounded by a lot of prejudice (as I described above). *The main problem is that the army is provided mostly for men's participation.* Both men and women resist in common, for the rights of all the people.

But it must be understood that the role of women in it is very important, because their position would be much worse if Russia seized power. Because the power of the aggressor is very conservative and sharply denies women's rights.

We have read that there is a strong feminist tradition, if not in that name, in Ukraine, of self-sufficient women resistant to patriarchal attitudes and norms. What truth is there to this vision? How does it show in the present mobilization of women against the Russian invasion?

Feminism in Ukraine is now a grassroots movement, run by activists. If you ask an average woman from the periphery what feminists are, she will answer something along the lines of 'These are some crazy young girls who have not developed a personal life, so they dye their hair in bright colours and hate men.' For example, my friend always tells me that feminists can only be young girls who don't have children and just want to find a community or a place to hang out. Obviously, there are a huge number of women with children in the feminist movement, but this attitude persists.

I think that this non-mass popularity of feminism is due to economic and social prerequisites: women have to work, look after children, provide for them somehow, and be a housewife (the stereotype that a woman is the keeper of the home is not going away). In the constant race for survival, you need to have the time and energy to be part of a movement / organisation / community.

It is indeed said about women in Ukraine (and they say it about themselves) that they are very strong, able to take a lot into their own hands, work hard and climb heights. But, as I mentioned before, they very often take that for granted.

Amid all the events and volunteering, the work of feminist organizations with women has increased dramatically. *It is also important that in addition to feminist organizations, there are organizations in which women play a leading role, and which are essentially fighting for women's rights in certain aspects (such as labour rights – I want to mention the nurses' union Be Like Nina.*

I believe this will help us build trust and show that feminism is about fighting for our rights and our self-determination.

The strongest component of the Russian anti-war movement is Feminist Anti-War Resistance, whose Telegram channel carries regular reports of what is really happening in Ukraine, including correspondence from women in the areas temporarily occupied by Russian forces. How is the Ukrainian movement looking to collaborate with its Russian sisters?

I follow the activities of this movement and consider these girls to be the only adequate leftists in Russia. While the once popular leftists are either splitting up or continuing to tell old narratives about the USSR and the 'fraternal peoples' and shoot videos on YouTube, these girls are engaged in underground activities and newspapers, putting up flyers, writing critical materials. I think that this is an important point for a totally *fragmented Russian society, where everyone is for himself or herself.*

Many female members of Feminist Anti-War Resistance signed the manifesto of Ukrainian feminists that I wrote together with my comrades.

I cannot make any predictions about further interaction. It is important to understand that Ukrainian feminist initiatives are also going through difficult times. In the light of military events very many people do not even want to hear about having any kind of cooperation with anything Russian. And here everything will depend on how the situation develops.

What are the most important issues that feminists in the rest of the world need to understand about the struggle of their sisters against the Russian invasion of Ukraine?

We have seen many pacifist statements by Western feminists, including their manifesto. In the face of war and the daily deaths of our women and children, we are critical of this position. In this context, I am part of a working group of Ukrainian feminists who have written the 'Ukrainian Feminist Manifesto'. We call for support for Ukrainian women, including our right to armed resistance. *This war shows us that feminism is a movement that needs to respond to changing situations, to be flexible and to develop principles according to new conditions.* What I mean here is that succumbing to geopolitical reasoning and geopolitical thinking and withdrawing from conflict by condemning all sides is not a workable position. We must clearly distinguish the rapist from the victim and help the victim to assert her right to exist and to be a subject.

Is there anything else you would like to add?

Our main goal now is to win this war. We understand that it can be protracted, and it is not a quick process, and there are hopes for it. *What is critical to victory is not to let the war and all the terrible events in Ukraine disappear from the world's agenda.* If everyone conditionally gets used to it, it will be harder for us to survive and the problem will not only be ours – there is a risk to the world, too. I ask you to support one of the Social Movement's biggest campaigns, for writing off Ukraine's foreign debt. It is a great burden for the Ukrainian economy, which has been created by years of oligarchical dominance. We have created a website where we have gathered arguments, a petition, and materials from around the world in support. It's important for women, too, because we will be the ones rebuilding Ukraine.

I want to say that women are already doing a lot to make Ukraine recover. And we, as a leftist organization, are fighting for our labour and social rights, which the government is trying to curtail to various degrees. This is important for the post-war rebuilding of Ukraine to be possible and based on the principles of non-discrimination.

This interview with Viktoriia Pihul by Dick Nichols was first published on 13 July 2022 by *Links International Journal of Socialist Renewal*, at www.links.org.au/ukraine-feminist-viktoriia-pihul-our-main-goal-now-is-to-win-this-war

Appeals from Ukrainian Trade Unions

On Saturday 9 April 2022, a demonstration took place in London called by eight national trade unions – Unions Stand with Ukraine. It was supported by both trade union federations of Ukraine. Published below are the statements from the Confederation of Free Trade Unions (KVPU) and the Federation of Trade Unions of Ukraine (FPU).

Message from *Mykhailo Volynets*, Chairperson of the Confederation of Free Trade Unions of Ukraine

Dear Brothers and Sisters,
The members of the Confederation of Free Trade Unions of Ukraine are grateful to you for your support and attendance at the solidarity rally in London.

This is the horrific war in Ukraine, during which the Russian Forces disregard the rules of war and commit war crimes and crimes against humanity.

This war is aimed to kill the people of Ukraine that chose freedom, democracy, and dignity and it is aimed to totally destroy the country that they have developed and built.

The Russian forces attack enterprises and agricultural objects to destroy the Ukrainian economy and cause poverty and even food crises and famine.

Bucha, Irpin, Motyzhyn, Vorzel, Borodyanka, Dymer, Dmytrivka… All these towns near the capital of Ukraine were not very well known in the world before. There were people who lived in peace, worked honestly, and made plans for the future. Now, these cities of the Kyiv region are symbols of the inhuman atrocities of the Russian Armed Forces. After these cities' liberation, the world knew about the horrific crimes of the Russian occupiers.

However, the bombing of hospitals and civil objects, executions, atrocities, raping, kidnapping, and forcible deportation are part of Russian inhumane tactics. The Russian troops are cynically ignoring all the rules of war and international humanitarian law, as well as the principles of humanity. Only in besieged and destroyed by airstrikes Mariupol at least 5000 civilians were killed, including 210 children.

This nightmare is a reason why there are more than 4 million, including 2 million refugee children, who fled from Ukraine and more than 6 million became Internally Displaced Peoples. These women, children, people with disabilities and pensioners fled from death, violence, and destruction. Please welcome them to the UK and your cities and help them.

Today workers and members of the KVPU work under the bullets and shellings and their families hide in basements in occupied cities. Our brave medical workers save lives of civilians and soldiers. Our railways and transport workers evacuate people from battle zones and carry cargo despite the shellings. The members of the KVPU help people with food, water, medicine and goods, and organize shelters and evacuations for women and children. Also, the members of the KVPU left their workplaces and homes and now are servicemen and servicewomen defending their Homeland from Russian occupiers.

Today the people of Ukraine do all possible to defend their Homeland. We all unite in the fight for freedom, democracy and independent

But the people of Ukraine need your help to win.

Ukraine needs assistance, primarily military, financial, and humanitarian aid. The KVPU calls to provide this assistance to Ukraine and to impose tougher sanctions on the Russian Federation.

We call for Russia to be punished severely for crimes against humanity and genocide in accordance with the UN Convention on the Prevention and Punishment of the Crime of Genocide, the Statute of the International Military Tribunal, and the Rome Statute of the International Criminal Court.

Russia must be stopped immediately! Putin's fascist criminal regime wants to destroy the people of Ukraine and also threatens peace and stability in Europe and the world.

Stand with Ukraine! Help the people of Ukraine to win in the struggle for independence and peace!

Message from *Grygorii Osovyi*, President of the Federation of Trade Unions of Ukraine

Stop Putin! No to the War against Ukraine!
Trade unions for Peace!

Dear brothers and sisters,
The whole world has stood up for Ukraine, condemning Russia's insidious aggression. The British unions stand beside our long-suffering people and the Ukrainian unions. For only together can we stop the deadly war.

The main task for all of us remains to defend our country, save people and bring victory closer.

Today is the 45th day of the heroic defence of our state and protection of our independence, freedom and democracy. The Ukrainians' right to be in the fraternal family of European society, not in the totalitarian Russian empire.

All these days the Russian invaders are trying to destroy the Ukrainian people, to raze Ukrainian cities and villages to the ground. But we will resist. And we will fight harder, the more they will attack. We will not give the enemy a single inch of Ukrainian soil, and the enemy must know it.

Many of our members have been forced to leave their jobs and take up arms to defend their families, their children and their land. Many of them, including trade unionists who in the early days of the war, took up arms and died. But we will always remember them.

We know that the road to victory is not yet close. We will have to go through gruelling missile attacks and air raids, because we still have the sky open to Russian attacks.

We will not allow our independence to be broken, just as you once did not want to lose it when the Nazis tried to take over your country.

We are grateful to the people, the UK government, who have provided us with invaluable humanitarian and military aid. However, we would ask for even stronger sanctions against Russia, which my country has deemed a terrorist state. Do the same. Recognize it as a terrorist state. Help secure our Ukrainian sky. Help defeat the global evil.

In addition to sanctions, which until there is peace should only increase, we would ask for economic support for Ukraine, funding for priority projects that will help restore employment. I believe that British unions can do much in this direction.

We are grateful to you for welcoming our refugees, who have been forced by this war to flee their homes, scattered to different countries and separated from their children.

But in any case, we are already thinking today about the future. About how we will rebuild Ukraine, where everyone will be happy, where everyone will live in peace. Thank you for bringing this future closer. Thank you for your solidarity.

Unions Strive to Keep Ukraine's Mines Running, Protect Civilians and Appeal for Solidarity

Interview with Nataliya Levytska, Deputy Chairperson of the NGPU (Independent Mineworkers Union of Ukraine), by Christopher Ford, Ukraine Solidarity Campaign.

Please explain your own position in the NGPU. How many workers do you represent; where do they work; and in which areas of Ukraine?

The independent trade union of miners of Ukraine (NGPU) represents mine workers in coal, iron and uranium ore, non-ferrous metals, peat and energy. It has representation in the regions of Donetsk, Luhansk, Dnipropetrovsk, Kirovohrad, Chernihiv, Zhytomyr, Rivne, Volyn, Ivano-Frankivsk and Lviv – a total membership, as of January 1, 2022, of 43,500 people. At the 9th NGPU Congress of May 27, 2021 I was elected to the post of first deputy chairperson. I have been working in independent trade unions for more than 20 years. The NGPU, together with members of trade union organizations, fights for the rights of miners, preservation of jobs, prevention of deterioration of labour legislation and social protection of miners and their families.

What is the NGPU trade unions' view of Russia's war on Ukraine?

The NGPU and our leading organizations consider Russia's attack to be a cynical attempt by the Russian regime to destroy Ukraine and its people. From the first days of the full-scale invasion, many miners voluntarily went to defend the Ukrainian land in the territorial defences and the Armed Forces of Ukraine. Most of our members volunteer and help civilians, the military and medics. We consider the Russian-Ukrainian conflict a war against democracy not only in Ukraine, but also in Europe and the world, as well as a genocide of the Ukrainian people.

There was already war in Donbas since 2014, how has the situation changed there with the full-scale Russian invasion in February?

In 2014 Russia attacked Ukraine and occupied part of the territories of Donbas. Some of the mines ended up in the occupied territory and actually stopped work. Miners and their families were forced to leave their homes and flee because they were in danger. The activities of the NGPU were banned by the occupation authorities of the so-called 'DNR' and 'LNR' and In May 2014 our leaders in Novogrodivka were kidnapped and tortured.

At the same time, mines on Ukrainian-held territory were still working so miners there had jobs and provided for their families. In the territory of Donbas, controlled by the Ukrainian government, local and central authorities invested in the development of local communities, with reconstruction of schools and hospitals. New jobs were created, children's and sports grounds were built, together with new parks and squares while hospitals and schools received modern equipment. But on February 24 changed everything.

Lysychansk, Severodonetsk, Popasna, Rubizhne and other cities of Luhansk region were actually destroyed by Russian troops. Almost the entire territory of Luhansk region is occupied. Most of the residents of the region became refugees, while others ended up in Russian filtration camps. All industrial enterprises were destroyed. There is no electricity, gas, or water supply in the cities. Most of the buildings have been destroyed and the housing stock is unusable. Fighting continues in the Luhansk region and the enemy uses air bombs, rockets and prohibited types of weapons.

Fierce battles continue in the Donetsk region, and our members are heroically defending it as well. Most of the cities of Donetsk region are subjected to bombings and rocket attacks every day in which civilians die. Cities turn into ruins. Mines are subjected to shelling and forced to stop work. The infrastructure of the region is being destroyed by the Russian invaders – schools, hospitals, kindergartens, churches, cultural institutions. With the impossibility of preparing for the cold season, the authorities announced the evacuation of residents of the Donetsk region but the miners have worked on heroically in the mines despite the threat to their lives due to shelling.

What was the situation of mineworkers before the invasion, were mines and industry functioning?

Mines and industrial enterprises in the territory of Donetsk and Luhansk regions held by Ukraine were working. The workers had a job and a salary. Even if there were delays in the payment of salaries to the miners.

Have mines stopped working since the invasion began?

In Luhansk region, all seven mines stopped working. Some were damaged by shelling, some were flooded, but the full picture is unknown because the territories are occupied by Russia. And what consequences it will have for the region's ecology is also unknown.

In the Donetsk region, two mines in Vugledar stopped working because they were destroyed by shelling. Others are operational but are close to the war zone.

What has been the impact of war on conditions of life in the mining communities, especially in East and Southern Ukraine?

The war changed the life of every citizen of Ukraine. We live in the conditions of war every day and every night and when we hear the warning sirens we do not know where and when Russia will use its weapons against us. Russia not only kills the population, including children, but also tries to psychologically break the Ukrainian people who are resisting and defending their democratic rights.

Are civilians and civilian areas being deliberately attacked by Russian forces?

I am convinced that Russia deliberately attacks civilian targets and the population, destroying all infrastructure and life support facilities. In addition, medical and school equipment, industrial equipment, grain and everything that is left is taken out of the captured territories. For example, even playground equipment was taken from Mariupol.

The KVPU, of which the NGPU is a member organization, constantly provides assistance to hospitals that have been damaged or looted by Russian troops. We are grateful to our brothers and sisters from other trade unions and partners for their help in this. Also, our local organizations in Donetsk and Dnipropetrovsk regions provide assistance to hospitals – from baby food to equipment and generators.

Russia appears to be trying to terrorize the population – how have Russian tactics affected the will of Ukrainians to resist?

Ukrainians have rallied and are trying to defend with all their might. Terror only increases resistance and hatred of enemies. Everyone is doing everything to bring victory closer: the population helps the Armed Forces, collects funds, organizes volunteer units and uses the smallest opportunities to resist the enemy. Even children are active participants in the volunteer movement.

Imagine that for the seventh month We live with constant alarm signals, destruction of our cities and threats of a nuclear disaster from Russia. Some of our members lose their loved ones to airstrikes and shelling while others who have become soldiers die in combat.

Despite this, Ukrainians continue to fight. International support helps us in this, because it shows that the whole world is with us.

Has there been a mobilization within mining communities to organize and assist each other since the invasion?

Of course, everyone helps each other. A family of miners from Donetsk and Luhansk regions found protection in Lviv and Volyn regions. Miners from Donbas were employed at the mines of the Dnipropetrovsk region.

As I already mentioned, we also help medical institutions. Moreover, we will provide humanitarian assistance to all those who need it, not only our members. The head of the NGPU, Mykhailo Volynets, often takes essential items to Donbas, Kharkiv, and Chernihiv regions himself.

Alongside the Ukrainian Army, are the territorial defence forces, and other battalions in mining and industrial areas mostly composed of workers?

Members of the NGPU take an active part in the fight against the enemy. Some were mobilized into the Armed Forces of Ukraine, others joined the ranks of territorial defence, the rest became participants in voluntary formations for the protection of territories. Until February 24, these people worked in mines, mined coal, and made plans. And today they protect the country. Unfortunately, we also have casualties among the mobilized miners. Yes, more than 20 miners from DC 'Lvivcoal' State Enterprise have already died at the front, there are also miners from other state-owned coal mining enterprises who have died.

In addition, our NGPU members work to ensure the energy independence of Ukraine.

In the local mobilizations to provide aid and organize defence, is there a significant involvement of women alongside men?

Women defend the country together with men. According to the Ministry of Defence, 5,000 women are on the first line of defence. In addition, women play a major role in the volunteer movement.

Our members volunteer in Donbas, Dnipropetrovsk, and Kirovohrad regions. Even those who are currently forced refugees in Europe are trying to help: they collect funds, buy and hand over medicines and supplies for the military, and help to organize support for Ukraine in European cities.

What has been the role of the NGPU since the invasion began?

From the first days of the full-scale invasion, the members of the NGPU actively participated in the defence of the country. In addition, NGPU members work extracting coal that the country needs.

Also, the NGPU immediately began to use its resources to help the affected communities and defenders. We are grateful for the help we receive from our brothers and sisters, because now our work opportunities have decreased due to the destruction of the economy and the growing unemployment. Russia is deliberately destroying our businesses and infrastructure in order to destroy our state, as well as – to get rid of a competitor in global markets.

Is the NGPU organizing aid and assistance to families in the mining communities?

The NPGU provides humanitarian assistance to miners and their families, helps them to evacuate to safe cities and provides other necessary assistance.

Are all trade unions organizing to defend Ukraine from the invasion?

Today, all citizens of Ukraine, including members of all trade unions, are making maximum efforts to fight the enemy and bring Victory closer.

There was previously some division between trade unions in Ukraine. Has the war led to greater solidarity across Ukraine amongst trades unions?

There may be differences between the unions and beyond, but now we are united in the fight against the enemy.

Russia claims they are fighting to 'liberate' Donbas and other areas from 'Nazis'? How do you respond to this allegation?

There have never been Nazis in Ukraine and there are none. There are no right-wing radical parties in the Ukrainian parliament. Both world politicians and celebrities come to Ukraine, and they see it for themselves. We do not need protection and liberation from anyone. Russia used 'Nazism' for propaganda purposes and as a pretext for an attack.

Ukrainians are a friendly, hardworking and free nation. We never attacked anyone. And if we see that the government is doing something wrong, we go to Maidan and resolve all issues. No aggression will stop our European and democratic aspirations.

Among the Russian forces there appear to be extreme right wing fascist groups. What is the politics of the Russian forces, including the so-called Donetsk Peoples' Republic?

All those who fight against Ukraine on our territory are fascists, whom we call racists. What they are doing on our land is worse than what happened during the Second World War. By the way, people who survived the Second World War are surprised by the current atrocities of the Rashists.

Russia also suggests that there is a threat to the Russian language in Ukraine, and of 'genocide' against Russian and Russian speakers?

This is pure delusion. In Ukraine, people have always been able to speak the language they are comfortable with. There was no oppression of Russian-speaking citizens. As a person who was born and grew up in the Donbass and spoke Russian, I never felt oppressed for my language. But now even Russian-speaking citizens are trying to switch to the Ukrainian language.

How has the war impacted on how people think about Ukrainian language and national identity?

We are proud to be Ukrainians and we all try to speak Ukrainian.

What is the current situation in the occupied areas of Ukraine?

According to the information of our members who remained in the occupied territory, the situation is difficult. In Donbas, men are afraid to go outside because they are being forcibly mobilized into the Russian army. They catch people with a pro-Ukrainian position, forcing them to get Russian passports. Those who refuse are subjected to torture. All are passed through filtration camps. Also, the Ukrainian language and education in schools in line with the Ukrainian curriculum are prohibited in the occupied territories. Residents of the occupied territories are waiting for the Armed Forces of Ukraine, but they do not talk about it openly. There is also a resistance movement in these territories.

Is there a free trade union movement in occupied areas?

No.

With a growing economic recession, some people in the UK have argued that there should be a cease-fire and peace now – how do you respond to such a position?

We want peace, but we are not ready to give up our territories. In 2014, we ceded Crimea, then part of Donbas, without firing a single shot, but this not only did not lead to peace, it led to a full-scale war on Ukrainian soil. We already know that Russia does not adhere to any agreements. Therefore, we will fight to Victory and we really hope that the whole world will support us. Because we are fighting not only for ourselves, but also for every European country.

Do you think a peace which involves partition of Ukraine is acceptable?

Ukraine is a free, independent country. We don't want anyone to divide us, and we won't allow it.

There is already discussion about the reconstruction of Ukraine after the war. Do you think the current struggle for national liberation should also have social objectives?

We must rebuild a social, European Ukraine. Our objective for the social reconstruction of Ukraine should be a decent salary, quality jobs, safe working conditions and social justice. And trade unions must always be an effective tool for protecting the rights of employees.

The Ukrainian parliament is processing laws which will significantly undermine employment rights and workers conditions, such as Draft Law 5371. What is your view of these new laws?

New laws must meet international and European standards, protect workers and create new jobs. We are now fighting against Draft Law 5371 and other bills that violate workers' rights.

What do you believe is the motive for these changes?
Perhaps certain representatives of the authorities believe that if they deregulate labour relations, they will increase investments in the country. But it is not so. The deterioration of labour legislation will have a negative impact on the post-war economy of Ukraine.

Do you think these changes can be reversed?
We will do our best to make it happen.

What solidarity can trade unions in the United Kingdom provide for you?
We will be grateful for any solidarity support and help.

Should we campaign for the British Government to send more weapons to Ukraine?
It must be so, because our defence and our Victory depend on the number of weapons.

We are supporting your appeal for assistance – Can you explain what specific aid is needed to help the mineworkers' resistance?
Ukrainians, including miners, need humanitarian and military aid. Any help would be greatly appreciated. For example, the members of the NPGU who defend the country need vehicles, unmanned aerial vehicles, thermal imagers, medical equipment, long-term storage and quick-cooking products. And the mining families who were forced to move to other regions need warm clothes, heaters, generators and food. Together with the support of our trade union brothers and sisters, we will definitely win!

Ukraine's Recovery Must Benefit the People: The West Has Other Ideas

Vitalii Dudin

The Ukraine Recovery Conference in Lugano aims to bring together government and business to discuss investment and the necessary reforms to support it.

Russia's war against Ukraine has not only left thousands dead and displaced – it's also presented an extreme challenge to Ukraine's economic well-being. And it is workers who are shouldering the cost.

While Ukrainian employers are dealing with the destruction of property and infrastructure, more than 80 per cent of workplace deaths have been caused by the Russian military since 24 February. One person dies at work in Ukraine every day – including railway workers, medical staff and other public sector workers – according to official data.

Ukraine is expected to lose an estimated 50 per cent of its GDP this year due to the Russian invasion. Hundreds of companies have been destroyed, and as a result, 30 per cent of jobs have been lost. According to the *Financial Times*, by the end of the year the unemployment rate in Ukraine will be at 25 per cent – a record in Europe.

So far, Ukrainian employers have been given a free hand to deal with the challenges of the Russian invasion. State agencies have loosened their oversight of the labour market.

And reformers in the parliament and government have sought to push through radical labour reforms that would strip Ukrainian workers of their rights.

But as millions of people try to figure out how to survive Ukraine's economic downturn, there's another question that looms on the horizon: what will happen when the war ends?

The future balance of economic power and prosperity in the country is likely to be determined by the changes being wrought in Ukraine now.

The coming demographic change

Russia's war has predictably reduced labour costs in Ukraine. In May, wages fell by an average of 10 per cent compared to the pre-war period. Advertised wages for jobs in areas such as raw material extraction, security and manual labour have almost halved.

There is a growing perception that the negative effects of the labour market crisis are being felt more by workers than by employers. Ukrainians were ready to endure any difficulties in the immediate aftermath of the Russian invasion. But as the tide of the war has changed, not everyone thinks the current situation – where business has advantages over workers – is fair.

This advantage has been expressed in the Ukrainian parliament's decision to revoke considerable parts of Ukraine's labour legislation for Ukrainian employers. Most importantly, employers are able to suspend employment contracts: in these cases, employees do not receive wages, but are still considered employed. Thousands of employees of private companies have remained effectively unemployed for months even without an official reason because of lack of enforcement. As of 1 April 2022, roughly 5 million citizens applied for one-time income loss benefits – but as of the end of May, the registered number of unemployed people was 308,000, which is 16 times lower.

Ukraine has thus become even more of a paradise for 'shadow employers' who do not employ people officially.

Since the Russian invasion, the state has cancelled all labour inspections during war time and no longer monitors wage debts – a consistent problem for Ukrainian employees. Thousands of employees of private companies have remained effectively unemployed for months without an official reason.

At the same time, Ukraine is also dealing with the fact that 6 million people, the majority of them women, have left the country. In Europe, some people – though far from everyone – have found themselves in countries where wages are higher, laws are obeyed, and housing and kindergartens are affordable. The return of young mothers to work in relatively peaceful cities is unlikely.

Sociologists predict that after the end of martial law, which currently forbids men under the age of 60 from leaving the country, Ukraine could face a new wave of emigration – where men will go abroad for work, to reunite with their families or to find safety from the ongoing conflict.

To help prevent this demographic change from becoming permanent, Ukraine will need to consider its socio-economic policy – to encourage people to stay in the country, rather than leave.

Reconstruction or anti-utopia?

Tasks such as rebuilding infrastructure, launching industrial production and meeting human needs can be addressed within the broad socio-humanitarian context of reconstruction.

But although there are international best practices, including from the International Labour Organization, it is unlikely that Ukraine's reconstruction will take into account the views of the population and its long-term interests.

So far, reconstruction plans for Ukraine have largely followed neoliberal traditions. One plan, drafted by Ukrainian government officials, leading experts and business associations, draws heavily on the principles of deregulation and liberalisation. Undoubtedly, these principles will be the basis

of the so-called analogue of the 'Marshall Plan' th
proposed to European partners.

In the meantime, though, some steps are alr(
implemented by the Ukrainian government. For example,
after Russia's destruction of big industrial enterprises, the state
wants to focus on the development of microbusinesses as a way
of relaunching the economy. The Ukrainian government's
proposals for reconstruction boil down to lending to micro-
entrepreneurs or training people in IT skills. Such steps may
have worked in peacetime, but today the development of self-
employment will be hampered by the destruction of Ukraine's
infrastructure, low purchasing power and general instability.
These structural factors can prevent small businesses from
setting up supply chains and finding their consumers.

The larger plan to be presented in Lugano this week will
likely be based, at least in part, on ideas found in 'A Blueprint
for the Reconstruction of Ukraine', published by a group of
international economists in April.

This blueprint plans 1) to introduce more flexible
employment contracts and eliminate labour legislation that
precludes the development of liberal economic policy; 2) to
provide government subsidies in order to attract foreign
companies; 3) large-scale privatization, including Ukraine's
biggest banks; 4) priority credit support for the export sector;
5) use of low-skilled and labour-intensive public works to fix
infrastructure; 6) to establish a technocratic agency that will
distribute international aid.

The main risks are that privatization and reduction of
civil servants may destroy protected jobs, and that newly
created ones will be precarious. There is also a threat that
infrastructure projects will simply enrich foreign corporations, and that the Ukrainian economy will retain its mostly
extractive nature instead of developing new innovative
industries. Ignoring the role of workers' organizations in the
reconstruction process will only intensify the problems of
shadow employment, unemployment and inequality.

There are, however, alternatives to consider for Ukraine's reconstruction. Ultimately, the aim should not be to rebuild peripheral capitalism, but to introduce elements of the social and solidarity economy in the country:

1 *Sustainable economic basis.* Priority should be given to the construction of production facilities and infrastructure that will create protected jobs at scale, improve the technological level of the economy and focus on domestic demand as opposed to exports. The main investor should be a state which is capable of mobilizing the necessary resources.

2 *Increased public confidence.* In order for money to be directed in the right direction, the whole of Ukrainian society should be involved in the decision-making process. There is a need for trade unions to support infrastructure projects and priorities for investment.

3 *Secured employment.* Abolish the war-time law that gives Ukrainian employers the right to suspend their obligations arising from individual and collective agreements. Provide labour inspectors with the necessary resources and powers to exercise oversight over the Ukrainian workplace. Mass public works should be accompanied with skill development for workers in order to improve their career prospects. There should be subsidies for Ukrainian enterprises that employ vulnerable groups, increase wages or involve trade unions in decision-making.

Private business has proved to be extremely irresponsible during the crisis. Post-war Ukrainian society needs integration, and that will be ensured by the development of state-owned and cooperative enterprises that do not make profits to the detriment of society and environment.

Ukraine faces a colossal task in dealing with huge destruction and re-launching industry, but neoliberal policies are not suitable for this. A strategy based on government intervention in the economy and the financing of employment programmes is needed. This, in turn, requires policies of redistribution through taxation and the confiscation of surplus wealth from Ukraine's richest people. This would be a concrete expression of Ukraine's long-promised policy of de-oligarchization, which has, it seems, faded from the political agenda since the beginning of the war.

In the short term, Russia's war has weakened Ukrainian workers' power. But in the long run, Ukraine's labour movement may intensify and improve employment conditions. Despite all the pessimism, Ukrainian society does have a belief in a more just model of reconstruction.

'Ukraine's Recovery Must Benefit the People' was first published on 4 July 2022 by *Open Democracy*, www.opendemocracy.net/en/odr/ukraine-rebuild-liberal-reforms-trade-unions

Resistance and Reconstruction: Issues for the Post-war Recovery

A Parliamentary Briefing

The Russian invasion of Ukraine is recognized as the largest European conflict since World War II. Ukrainian resistance has been an inspiration and discussions are beginning on how best to organise Ukraine's post-war recovery.

The rebuilding of Ukraine will be one of the most challenging undertakings of the twenty-first century. The Ukraine Solidarity Campaign with Alex Sobel MP hosted a Parliamentary Briefing on key questions faced by Ukrainians and the UK regarding the reconstruction of a free Ukraine. This was held on 23 May with a range of speakers from Ukrainian civil society, the labour movement and the Ukraine Solidarity Campaign. This chapter comprises the text of briefings prepared by three of the speakers.

The speakers at the Briefing were: Mykhailo Volynets, Chairperson of the Confederation of Free Trade Unions of Ukraine; Vasily Andreev, Vice-Chairman of the Federation of Trade Unions of Ukraine; Dr Yuliya Yurchenko of Sotsialniy Rukh / Social Movement (Ukraine) and the University of Greenwich; Bohdan Ferens, Social Democratic Platform (Ukraine); Mick Antoniw MS, Counsel General and Minister for the Constitution; Dr Gregory Schwartz, University of Bristol.

Bohdan Ferens, founder member of the
Social Democratic Platform
Why does Ukraine deserve more?

1   Every day on my Facebook there are mentions of
    fallen heroes who defend Ukraine from Russian
    invaders. These are young male students, older male
    fathers and female volunteers. They made completely
    different plans for life four months ago, in which
    there was definitely no place for war and death. These
    are the new realities in which Ukrainians live. The
    price of freedom and the desire to become a full part of
    the European Community *is too high*. It is measured
    by tens of thousands of dead civilians, including more
    than *three hundred children killed by Russian troops*,
    destroyed cities and infrastructure. For two months
    and twenty-seven days in a row, the Armed Forces of
    Ukraine and the Ukrainian people have been resisting
    continued attacks by the Russian occupiers in various
    directions. The Russian troops are using methods that
    violate the rules of war. They attack civilian infra-
    structure, killing and injuring civilians, including
    children and women, and make actions that can have
    regional and international consequences.

2   The Kremlin brutally attacked Ukraine with explicitly
    imperialist aims, with a view to restoring what it
    considers its so-called rightful 'sphere of influence' in the
    post-Soviet space, thus implicitly threatening not only
    Eastern European Partner Countries but EU members
    and the UK. The aggression also entails a systemic
    element. Putin's Russia is promoting an autocratic-state
    model, using *Russism as an ideological superstructure* of
    military expansionism and nationality cult, in contrast
    to the democratic polity towards which countries such
    as Ukraine have been striving – the value system on
    which the EU is founded and which it seeks to project.

3   The *prerequisites* for the *end of the war* are not yet observed, so it is necessary to be prepared for a protracted confrontation and support for Ukraine in its struggle. This support primarily provides for the provision of weapons, financial and humanitarian assistance. The *position of the progressive left* in this regard should be very clear – *maximum support* for the Ukrainian people, since *Russian bombs and troops cannot be stopped only with the help of pacifism.* Diplomacy failed. This, unfortunately, must be stated as a fact. But any war sooner or later ends with a truce. Diplomatic efforts alone are not enough for achieving this goal. Putin understands only the language of force, and not only the future of Ukraine, but also a new system of European, and perhaps global security, will depend on the success of the Ukrainian army at the front.

4   The *reconstruction of Ukraine* must already begin. There is no need to wait for the end of the war to renew the infrastructure and rebuild the bombed-out cities. Tens of thousands of people need a roof over their heads, and children in many villages and cities that were under temporary occupation dream of starting the new school year in renovated schools. All these tasks cannot be carried out without the help of Western partners, including the UK, in the short and long term. *Rebuilding post-war Ukraine will require a lot of financial and human resources.* We need to be realistic and understand that not all Western partners will be ready to provide such resources. Domestic problems, the repercussions of the pandemic, the recession, and some weariness from the Russian war against Ukraine may prevent such assistance from being provided. In this regard, politicians, decision makers and citizens play a key role, as the level of support will depend on their involvement and empathy with Ukraine.

5   It is also necessary to take more *radical steps* that will allow Ukraine to overcome the financial and economic crisis. Such a step could be the *cancellation of sovereign debt*, or at least part of this debt, since the financial system was not particularly capable of covering external debts on loans in the pre-war period, and what can we say when there is a war. The provided monetary assistance should have a targeted application and a transparent monitoring distribution system. First of all, the *results of the use of this assistance should be seen by ordinary people* in the construction of residential buildings, bridges, the repair of social infrastructure, the provision of basic needs and social guarantees. New jobs must be created so that people who are already unemployed today can feed themselves and their families. Another serious problem is the decrease in the level of financial transfers from labour migrants (many men went to the front or cannot leave the country to work), which traditionally helped support the economy.

6   It is impossible to resolve all these problems without a *deep restructuring of Ukraine itself.* The political elites should get rid of the politicians of the past and oligarchs as much as possible, and Ukrainian society, which has gone through such difficult trials, should be more demanding of itself and those who are elected to defend their interests. There should be parties in parliament that will not only strengthen the defence sector and build up military power, but also *prioritize education and the social sphere,* protect labour rights and fight against the infringement of marginalized groups. In times of war, the most vulnerable always suffer. The *main task of the progressive left is not to live by the slogans of the past, but to try to act now,* in spite of any difficulties. *Trade unions* should also be modernized in Ukraine. Only new leaders and fresh

approaches can fill the trade union movement with new vitality in order to better protect worker's rights.

7   We are sincerely grateful to the British people for their help and solidarity at this difficult time. It would also be very helpful if the representatives of the *Labour Party* were more involved in support of Ukraine. Such support may include very practical actions such as a *visit to Ukraine,* support for legislative initiatives aimed at helping the Ukrainian people, increased *sanctions* against Russia, including Russian oligarchs, politicians and their families who own expensive real estate and assets in London, investigations of the links of Russian financial and industrial groups with the British political establishment. On the part of the sd Platform, we are ready to help in organizing a visit to Kyiv, as well as to deepen cooperation.

Mick Antoniw, member of the **Welsh Parliament**

I make this note for the meeting in a personal capacity. I am a Welsh Labour member of the Welsh Parliament / Senedd and hold the position of Counsel General and Minister of the Constitution in the Welsh Government.

1   The evidence of War Crimes committed by Russia and Russian Federations citizens or agents is over-whelming. Investigations are underway by the International Criminal Court and also by the United Nations.

2   The nature of the crimes includes conducting a war of aggression against a peaceful sovereign neighbour, as well as numerous examples of murder including planned liquidations, attacks on residential areas, use of prohibited weaponry, torture, rape, looting and others.

3   It is vital that the issue of the investigation of and accountability for war crimes does not become in any way negotiable. The upholding of international law in this area is fundamentally important. Any divergence

from this undermines the credibility and status of International Law. Those who commit war crimes, whoever and whatever their status must be held to account.

4 Reparations: Post war, Russia must be held to account for its actions as a state that has invaded and attacked a peaceful neighbour without cause. Those assets seized or frozen must become the basis of a package of post-war assets that can be allocated for the reconstruction of Ukraine and reparation to victims. This has to be addressed internationally but may require legislation at national level. It is important this process starts now.

5 The Law of the Sea must be guaranteed enabling the free passage of ships and goods to Ukrainian ports. The Russian blockade must be brought to an end and this may require international action.

6 Russian troops must be withdrawn from Ukraine and international sovereignty as guaranteed by International Law and the Budapest agreement must by re-established.

7 Only then can the issue of sanctions be discussed. Sanctions are the main international leverage. They must be upheld and indeed strengthened. Changes to the sanctions regime must be contingent on 1–6 above.

Yuliya Yurchenko, member of Sotsialnyi Rukh / Social Movement

On April 10 the World Bank updated its GDP prognosis for Ukraine to state that the Russian invasion was to shrink Ukraine's economy by 45% in 2022 alone – it will be larger by the end of this war, the final date is not clear. By March 29, 2022 already the country's direct one-off losses due to the invasion already exceeded $1 trillion, according to Prime Minister Shmygal. Even prior to the invasion Ukraine already was one of the poorest and most indebted countries in Europe. Current budgetary expenditure on arms, humanitarian needs, and medical needs of the wounded have grown exponentially.

There is growing recognition at international, EU and US governing body level, and acknowledgement in the IMF report of April 2022, that Ukraine will also need money to reconstruct its homes and infrastructure and clean up and decontaminate cities and countryside.

Post-World War II social and economic reconstruction experience as well as the last two years of pandemic responses present us with useful blueprints of actions that work in conditions of extreme exogenous shocks to economic systems. State-led investment, cross-sectoral support and cooperation, and 'fiscal activism' are the bedrock principles of the immediate, mid- and long-term response being successful. Fiscal activism is a highly effective set of measures aimed at stabilizing the economy by granting the state a wider spectrum of options with its budgetary expenditure and acting as an investor in its own economy sectors in order to lift it out of debris.

Ukraine is in a state of an unprovoked and uneven war and needs large-scale multi-faceted international assistance (military and financial) and we at Sotsialnyi Rukh welcome and express our deep gratitude for what has already been set in motion, including in the UK. We recognize too that assistance must be always used purposefully. For that we need Ukraine's state debt cancellation and facilitation of 'fiscal activism' of Ukraine's government for the foreseeable future. Assistance to a country in a state of war should be targeted at its urgent needs and not be used to prop up debt servicing, especially as some debt was accrued in odious circumstances, e.g. as a result of the 2013 agreement whereby Russia was to purchase Ukrainian Eurobonds, the legitimacy of which is currently being decided by the UK Supreme Court. Nor should the country be pushed to accrue more debts and thus again essentially misallocate the needed funds, as they should be spent supporting the population, rebuilding the country, its economy or lifting it out of the debris of war. International cooperation and oversight too are welcome and needed.

We ask you to support:

1 Suspension of debt servicing via coordinated effort of international institutions and statespersons (similar to the H.R.7081 – Ukraine Comprehensive Debt Payment Relief Act).

2 Work (Sotsialniyi Rukh / Social Movement) towards an international plan for full debt cancellation for Ukraine.

3 Support (Sotsialniyi Rukh / Social Movement) development of the post-war reconstruction plan collectively financed by reparations from Russia as well as those international partners willing to support Ukraine based on the post-World War II reconstruction experiences and the Covid-19 exogenous shock response lessons, first and foremost for key industries and on the principles of green, just transition, social dialogue, and energy democracy.

4 Support military aid for Ukraine, sanctions against Russia, and forfeiture of oligarchic assets towards reconstruction of Ukraine.

Why Should Ukraine's Debt Be Cancelled?

Interview with Eric Toussaint

Sushovan Dhar interviewed *Eric Toussaint* of the Campaign to Cancel the Illegitimate Debt.

How much is the Ukrainian public debt and who are the main creditors?

Ukraine's external debt, public and private, is about $130 billion, half of it owed by the government, and the other by the private sector. The government also has an internal debt of over $40 billion. Public external debt in the form of sovereign securities amounted to $20 billion in 2021, all of which (there were 14 issues of securities) are governed by English law, and in the event of a dispute the British courts can be called upon. In 2021, the debt to the IMF amounted to more than $13 billion. The debt to the World Bank (WB), the European Bank for Reconstruction and Development (EBRD) and finally the European Investment Bank (EIB) amounted to more than $8 billion. The amounts to be repaid in 2022 for both the external and internal debt are enormous and unsustainable in view of the war situation. And finally, there is Ukraine's bilateral external debt to China, France, Germany, other EU countries, the United States and a $3 billion debt to Russia. Since the beginning of the Russian invasion, Ukraine's public debt has increased significantly because the IMF and the World Bank have granted a new credit of $5 billion, and other multilateral financial institutions have also granted emergency credits.

And the government issued more than $2 billion in new debt securities, called war bonds.

What is the background of Ukraine's indebtedness?
Let me give you a short history of Ukraine's indebtedness since its independence, a little more than thirty years ago when the Soviet Union collapsed at the end of 1991. Ukraine did not inherit any debt from the Soviet Union, so it started in a favourable situation, but in the process of a brutal capitalist restoration, the Ukrainian bureaucrats who restored capitalism benefitted at the expense of the state coffers. Oligarchs got extraordinarily rich at the expense of state assets just as happened in the Russian Federation, Belarus, Kazakhstan, Tajikistan, etc. While a number of oligarchs were getting extraordinarily rich, they were supported by members of the government, who allowed them to acquire public property for a pittance. The government financed a large part of the budget with debt because the richest people in Ukraine hardly paid any taxes. The Ukrainian government systematically resorted to borrowing, including from private banks created by the oligarchs. While the oligarchs benefited from all kinds of aid from the state, they lent part of this money to the same state with an interest rate that allowed them to make large profits.

Did the government resort to external borrowing as well?
Yes, the government resorted to external borrowing. It issued debt securities on the international financial markets and also borrowed from foreign banks. It borrowed from the IMF and the World Bank. The debt steadily increased from the 1990s to the 2000s. The IMF set conditionalities while extending loans to Ukraine – the application of the shock strategy, with typical neo-liberal measures: liberalisation and promotion of foreign trade, removal of price control of essential commodities, reduction of subsidies on basic items

consumed by working people, the deterioration of a whole series of essential services. The IMF also promoted the rapid privatization of state-owned enterprises. It set tighter and tighter targets for the reduction of public deficit. The IMF has compounded the insecurity of the labour market by facilitating lay-offs in the private and public sectors. The effects of the policies recommended by the IMF have been disastrous – an extreme impoverishment of the population, so much so, that in 2015 Ukraine was at the bottom of the ladder of all European countries in terms of real wages.

Is an important part of the Ukrainian debt illegitimate?

The answer is yes: the overwhelming majority of the Ukrainian debt, if not all, is illegitimate. It was not contracted in the interest of the population; it was accumulated in the interest of the richest 1 per cent and international creditors; at the expense of a dramatic deterioration in the social rights and living conditions of the population. This took place before the outbreak of war and the Russian invasion of Ukrainian territory which took place twice, in 2014 and in February 2022.

Already before the two aggressions committed by the Russian Federation led by Vladimir Putin in 2014 and 2022, the debt claimed from Ukraine was a debt that did not benefit the population and it was absolutely normal to consider that this debt should not be repaid by the population.

Which parts of the debt should be cancelled as a priority?

The debt claimed by the IMF, which is by far the largest among multilateral debts, should be cancelled as it has played a direct role in the process of gradual destruction of the Ukrainian economy and in the drastic deterioration of the living conditions of a large section of the Ukrainian population. The IMF has also favoured the enrichment of the richest 1 per cent and fostered the rise of inequality.

A particular chapter must be opened in the context of the debt claimed by Russia from Ukraine. In December 2013, when Ukraine had Viktor Yanukovych as its president, who was closely linked to Putin's regime, the Russian Federation convinced Ukraine's Ministry of Finance to issue securities on the Dublin Stock Exchange in Ireland for an amount of $3 billion. This was the first issue that was supposed to be followed by others to gradually reach $15 billion. So, the first issue of securities amounted to $3 billion and all the securities sold in Dublin were bought by the Russian Federation through a private company it had set up in Ireland. The interest rate was 5 per cent. The following year, Russia annexed Crimea, which until then had been part of Ukraine. The Ukrainian government changed as a result of popular mobilizations, the exact nature of which is debatable as there was both a genuine popular rebellion and intervention by the right and extreme right. There was also the will of Western powers to take advantage of popular discontent. It's all quite complicated and I'm not in a position to make an analysis of the so-called Orange Revolution. The new government continued for a while to pay back the debt to Russia. In total, $233 million of interest was paid to Russia. Then in December 2015, the government decided to suspend the payment of the debt.

In brief, the Ukrainian government justified the suspension of payments by explaining that it had the right to take countermeasures against Russia because the latter had attacked Ukraine and annexed Crimea. And indeed, under international law, a state has the right to take countermeasures and suspend the fulfilment of a contract in such circumstances.

The Russian Federation took the case to the UK courts in London. Indeed, it was provided that the securities were issued in accordance with English law and that in case of dispute the British courts would have jurisdiction. Therefore, Russia filed a complaint against Ukraine asking the UK courts to order Ukraine to resume payment. The proceedings started in 2016. At the moment, the British courts have not yet delivered a final judgement, which should be pronounced in the next weeks or months.

There was a first judgment, followed by an appeal against the judgment. Then finally a session in the Supreme Court of the United Kingdom took place on 11 November 2021 (this session can be viewed in its entirety on the website of the Supreme Court of the United Kingdom)

It is worth noting that at first the British judges, notably the principal judge who was in charge at the beginning of the proceedings, was none other than William Blair, Tony Blair's brother, who had until recently very close business links with Putin's Russia. He tended to rule in favour of Russia since the UK judiciary wants to remain attractive to investors. Tony Blair's brother issued a judgement in March 2017 in which he did not accept a series of obvious arguments put forward by Ukraine. William Blair considered that there had been no real coercion of Russia by Ukraine. He considered that this was not a conflict between states. He accepted Russia's claim that the company that bought the Ukrainian securities (The Law Debenture Trust Corporation PLC) is a private entity. However, in reality, this company is acting directly on behalf of Russia and it is Russia that actually bought all the securities.

Subsequently, the Court of Appeal challenged William Blair's ruling and now the case has reached the final stages in the Supreme Court.

As Russia invaded Ukraine at the end of February 2022 with a huge loss of life and war crimes, it is difficult to foresee the Supreme Court siding with Russia against Ukraine in this case. The judgement will be heavily influenced by the dramatic turn of events in the conflict between Russia and Ukraine. If the Court recognizes that Russia has exercised duress against Ukraine and that Ukraine has the right to take counter-measures, this will set a precedent and other states will be able to invoke this precedent in their dispute with creditors. So, it's an important issue.

What is the CADTM's position on the cancellation of the Ukrainian debt?

The CADTM considers that all the debts claimed from Ukraine should be cancelled. These are the debts that are in the hands of private creditors and which represent 80 per cent of the external debt, the debts that are claimed by the IMF and the World Bank and other multilateral organisations, and the debts claimed by the states, which are called bilateral debts. The, CADTM in demanding the cancellation of the Ukrainian debt in this manner, joins an international petition which was launched after the invasion of Ukraine by social movements and individuals who are in Ukraine and resisting the invasion. The signatories of this petition rightly state: 'Chaotic borrowing and antisocial debt conditionality was a result of total oligarchization: unwilling to fight the wealthy, the state rulers kept getting deeper in debt. Loans were issued under conditions of social spending cuts, and their repayment forced [the government] to economize on vital needs and apply austerity to foundational economy sectors.' This is enough to demand the cancellation of the Ukrainian debt.

What is the Ukrainian government doing?

It is indeed very important to ask this question: what is the Ukrainian government doing? Instead of suspending all debt payments in order to meet the needs of the population and to resist external aggression, the Ukrainian government, in a purely neoliberal approach, is maintaining debt repayments, except for the debt claimed by Russia. We are therefore in an extremely serious situation. While the government ought to suspend payment of the debt, it is absolutely determined to remain credible in the eyes of the financial markets and the various lenders, and so it continues to allocate considerable sums of money from its budget to pay off the interest on the debt.

What this government also does is borrow more money. It issues war bonds that are sold on the financial markets. So, the Ukrainian government is increasing the debt, and it has also increased its requests for credit from the IMF, the World Bank, the European Bank for Reconstruction and Development, the European Investment Bank and bilateral creditors. It continues to implement neo-liberal policies of anti-social austerity, arguing that extraordinary efforts are needed to achieve resistance to the Russian invasion. The government has decreed that workers must work longer; that they must take less leave; and it has made it easier for employers to lay off workers in the midst of a war situation. I think that the policy of the existing government needs to be denounced. We should adopt a completely different approach: suspending the payment of the debt, asking the country where the assets of the Ukrainian oligarchs are located to expropriate these assets and return them to the Ukrainian people. Of course, it is also necessary to expropriate the Russian oligarchs and transfer their assets to a reconstruction fund for Ukraine under the control of social movements. But, while the international press focuses precisely on the Russian oligarchs, there is no reason for the CADTM to consider that the Ukrainian oligarchs are allies of the Ukrainian people. The class struggle during the war continues. The Ukrainian oligarchs must be held accountable and expropriated while in reality, with the complicity of the Ukrainian government and foreign powers, they continue to enrich themselves in an absolutely shameful manner.

The Ukrainian government should also impose a war tax on the richest 1 per cent to finance the war effort. An audit of the debt should be carried out with the participation of the citizens because the debt has reached such proportions that it is absolutely inconceivable not to name those responsible for the totally reckless indebtedness carried out by the previous and current governments.

'Why Should Ukraine's Debt Be Cancelled?' was first published on 21 April 2022 by the Committee for the Abolition of Illegitimate Debt, www.cadtm.org/Why-should-Ukraine-s-debt-be-cancelled

Campaign success:
Cancel Ukraine's Debt update from Debt Justice,
21 July 2022

- Ukraine's lenders have agreed to campaigners' demands to suspend the country's debt repayments for around two years. This will free up billions of dollars to enable the Ukrainian people to address the severe humanitarian crisis and costs of the Russian invasion.
- The Ukrainian government yesterday requested that government creditors and bondholders agree to a suspension of repayments until the end of 2023, extendable by another year.
- The Group of Creditors of Ukraine, including the UK, the USA and Germany, responded by agreeing to the request and strongly encouraging bondholders to consent.
- Ukraine has now received explicit indications of support from its main private lenders including BlackRock.
- Ukraine was due to spend $7.3 billion in debt repayments in 2022 alone.
- We have been campaigning for a debt suspension for Ukraine since March, alongside Ukrainian social movement Sotsialnyi Rukh, the Ukraine Solidarity Campaign and Another Europe.
- MPs Caroline Lucas (Green), Chris Law (SNP) and Richard Burgon (Labour) were powerful advocates for debt relief for Ukraine in the UK Parliament.
- This breakthrough shows how campaigning can help to convert the unthinkable into the inevitable. Thank you to everyone who has supported this campaign – whether it's signing our petition, sharing our articles or helping us to spread the word. You have helped to push this issue onto the political agenda.
- The Ukrainian government and its Western allies had previously insisted that it would pay its debts, and

repayments to bondholders have continued throughout the invasion. Only last week the IMF insisted that it expected Ukraine to continue to pay.

- In the long term, the struggle will continue to ensure that, once the war is over, the debt of a free Ukrainian government is cancelled, so that all available resources can be dedicated to what will be a massive reconstruction effort. It seems highly unlikely that Ukraine will restart paying off its creditors after the end of the war – eventual debt cancellation should be inevitable.
- These developments will increase the pressure on the G20 to apply a similar level of political will to resolving the debt crises facing other lower income countries such as Zambia and Sri Lanka.

This update was first published at
www.debtjustice.org.uk/news/campaign-success-cancel-ukraines-debt

Reinventing Nazism for State Propaganda: How Morality is Being Replaced by Force

Ilya Budraitskis

llya Budraitskis explains how the Kremlin understands 'de-Nazification' and how this interpretation is driving the war in Ukraine. In the Kremlin's terms, the difference between Nazi and non-Nazi comes down to alien versus your own

It's evident that the Kremlin isn't pursuing only geopolitical goals in Ukraine, like restoring 'historical Russia' or containing NATO. The speeches of Vladimir Putin, as well as the official propaganda, point to an ambitious ideological goal – the complete revision of the political and moral concepts underpinning the European consensus since World War II. The core of that decades-long unspoken consensus can be encapsulated in the laconic 'never again / nie wieder.' The assumption was that the page in history in which Nazism was possible as an ideology and a system of practices, had been forever been turned and that Nazism couldn't return in any form. For decades the foundation of this assumption was collective memory, which stood above any national borders and couldn't become the object of any conflict in pursuit of state interests. However, generations changed. Memories lost their vividness. All that remained of Nazism was its status as an absolute evil that couldn't be justified. Yet it was in this very status that Nazism was turned into a key justification for Russia's war against Ukraine.

Putin's 'denazification' meant first and foremost that the war was not only acceptable but morally necessary. In a war against Nazism there can't be any compromises, and the price to be paid doesn't matter. In the battle between good and evil a peaceful settlement can't be reached as it would only lead to the good side being corrupted and spoiled. Nazism defied all human laws and thus the Nazis themselves aren't to be granted any universal rights. Like with terrorists, you don't negotiate with Nazis – you kill them. Thus, if Ukraine has become a Nazi state, and the entire Western world collectively conspired for that to happen, then it is only Russia that can mete out moral justice. It thus receives the right to restore universal humanity, as the rest of mankind has lost its immunity to Nazism.

This is the monstrous logic of a recent article by Timofey Sergeytsev, which offers a moral justification for the massacres in Bucha. He writes that the fight against Nazism today has become a 'purely Russian affair' due to the 'anti-fascist nature' of 'Russian civilization'. In an equation where military strength equals morality, the opposite is also true: morality is determined by force. If Ukraine is 'denazified' as Sergeytsev proposes – through massacres and the 're-education' of the 'Nazified' population in concentration camps – then this is exactly what a victory of good over evil, in a new world free of Nazism, will look like. Or, as Sergeytsev puts it, 'the ideology of a denazifier cannot be disputed by the guilty party that is to be subjected to denazification.' The alternative is simple: either Nazism must be destroyed without pity or a 'new Holocaust' awaits Russians.

In her famous book *The Origins of Totalitarianism*, Hannah Arendt wrote that Hitler (unlike Stalin) is a 'new type of criminal' as he didn't seek justification in the distorted humanistic morality of the past but sought to establish a fundamentally new one. The new morality would wash away the very concept of man as such (and, accordingly, his natural rights) and replace it with a struggle of races as biological species created unequal by nature. The right to life and death is thus not universal, but constantly being dynamically redefined in the existential racial battle for living space.

Franz Neumann, another astute scholar of Nazism, analysed the deformation of Nazi Germany's judicial system, which was based on a 'phenomenological' approach to law. This means that the verdict in the Nazi court was passed on the basis of the essence and not the deed, primarily answering the question 'who', while 'what' was entirely secondary. The court thus did not take an impartial position but was merely an instrument for the protection of the race, shielding it from any threats to purity and internal unity. The relativity of morality and law to the laws of nature, turned upside down by the continuous political and military struggle of antagonistic racial 'entities', constituted a key element of Nazi ideology. It was this vision of reality that was defeated in World War II and that should never again be revived (it would inevitably give rise to new wars).

Nazism thus loses its universal features and turns into a tool to create 'the enemy'. The difference between Nazi and non-Nazi would come down to alien versus your own. And making that distinction depends only on brute force, naked military dominance. The biggest prize in the Ukraine war for Putin's Russia is the opportunity to label a Nazi anyone who refuses to submit to the dictate of the victor (and therefore deprive him of the right to exist).

If in World War II, as Putin believes, the Soviet Union was merely an avatar of the eternal 'historical Russia', then Russia is organically 'anti-fascist' and all its external opponents are potentially 'Nazis'. In this construction, the fight against the absolute evil of Nazism becomes one and the same as the struggle for global dominance by Russia. Morality and geopolitics merge into a fundamentally inseparable whole, and entire nations become carriers of ideas (good or evil) solely based on their 'essence' – their 'historical fate', which contemporaries can't alter.

The eclectic window-dressing – be it racial theory or 'de-Ukrainization' – is just a matter of specific historical circumstances. Those who believe that fascism is born out of a fanatical obsession by the masses with some 'big ideas' are deeply mistaken; on the contrary, fascism is based on the deepest cynicism and the utmost contempt for the ability of people to believe in ideas and pursue them to the end. After all, any idea or concept, according to fascism, is always just a trick in the animal struggle of interests: unlike all universal rights and freedoms, which are actually nothing more than hypocritical chatter, 'essence' ('racial instinct', 'human nature', 'cultural codes', etc.) never lies.

During his twenty years in power, Putin has consistently preached such cynicism, which has corroded society from top to bottom. Today the logical outcome of this unbridled cynicism is the ideological justification of war crimes and the dehumanization of an entire nation. Real denazification of Russia is a difficult task that lies ahead. A central element of it must be rethinking and addressing this dangerous mixture of contempt for the weak and apologizing for competition and violence, which is capable of reinvigorating Nazism again and again.

'Reinventing Nazism for State Propaganda' was first published in Russian at Republic.ru, and in English at www.anticapitalistresistance.org/reinventing-nazism-for-state-propaganda-how-morality-is-being-replaced-by-force

I Marched against Putin's War for the Same Reason I Protested the War in Iraq

Niko Vorobyov

I was born in Saint Petersburg, or Leningrad as we called it in the good old days. Until February 24, the last anti-war protest I attended was almost twenty years ago, back when George W. Bush and Tony Blair were planning the invasion of Iraq. I was a schoolboy in Britain, and we sat at the top of the football pitch and refused to go to class. True, most of us didn't understand the geopolitical situation too well – some were just trying to bunk off biology. But I knew enough to tell that if Saddam Hussein really did have weapons of mass destruction, surely that would be a good reason not to attack him?

With that experience in mind, earlier this year I also didn't believe all those warnings that Russia was about to invade Ukraine, coming from US spooks and the Pentagon. They had lied about Iraq – and I'm still anxiously awaiting Donald Trump's pee tape and who knows what else.

Then, on February 24, I found myself at another protest, except this time it was on Nevsky Prospekt in Saint Petersburg. Instead of angry teachers, we faced the OMON riot squad who dragged us away at random, including a mother carrying a baby and an elderly woman who survived the siege of Leningrad. That night, more than 1,700 people were arrested in fifty-three cities across Russia.

I could follow the logic in Russia bullying Ukraine into staying out of NATO. Let's not pretend the United States wouldn't threaten Armageddon if one of its neighbours joined a rival pact – just ask Cuba. And I could understand supporting the rebels. Ukraine has a complex national identity, and when the pro-Western uprising happened in 2014, it was presented as though 'the people had spoken', when many in the south and east saw events unfold rather differently.

I thought that way, right up until the bomb sirens sounded in Kyiv. I've been against all sorts of Western imperialism for a very long time, especially the American-imposed 'war on drugs'. So, it's frustrating when my comrades lap up my own motherland's lies about its blatantly imperialist war.

Liberating Russian speakers?

Vladimir Putin claims we're saving the Russian-speaking people of East Ukraine from genocide by the neo-Nazi Azov regiment. If this was truly about saving them, Russian peacekeepers could have secured the Donbas in a day. I'm no general, but I doubt the Ukrainians would be foolish enough to try anything then. Even if they had – for whatever absurd reason – truly wanted to commit 'genocide' on their own relatives, they wouldn't do it while hundreds of thousands of Russian soldiers are standing by and they know Washington hasn't got their back.

I harbour no illusions about Azov. I've interviewed Sergey Korotkikh – he's not a neo-Nazi, he's *the* neo-Nazi. The man literally founded the National Socialist Society, which carried out a racist skinhead murder spree in Moscow in the late 2000s. Now he's an Azov commander. But flattening Mariupol to smoke them out is the same excuse Israel rolls out each time they bombard Gaza: blow up an apartment block, then claim there were terrorists inside using 'human shields'. Do neo-Nazis exist in Ukraine? Yes. Is demolishing entire city blocks a reasonable and proportionate response? No.

And just as a certain Israeli prime minister said 'There was no such thing as Palestinians' – justifying decades of occupation and apartheid – so Putin has a bizarre delusion that Ukrainians don't exist either. They were just made up, by

Vladimir Lenin, apparently. Never mind the fact that we're supposedly fighting ultranationalists right now (of which nation, exactly?) seems to disprove that point.

And what about the long-suffering people of East Ukraine? Is Russia liberating them?

The United Nations observers, including Russia, reported over 3,000 civilian deaths in 2014–15, at the peak of the fighting in Donbas, but only eighteen by 2021. That's a lower rate of violent death than London's. If there was a concentrated effort to wipe out civilians by either side, it ended years ago. Yet right now, thousands of Russian speakers are dying in Ukraine, whereas they weren't when this 'special operation' began.

Again, look at Iraq. For some Iraqis, Saddam's regime was a golden age. For others, it was hell on Earth: besides gassing the Kurds, Saddam invaded his neighbours (in the case of Iran, with America's support), and human rights were a sick joke. Being against the war in 2003 didn't mean you admired him. It meant that a 'special operation' would bring even more death and suffering than there was already. Now Mariupol is rubble, and it wasn't that way before Russian 'help'.

To be sure, there was much about modern Ukraine that I, and many Russians, found toxic: the stubborn insistence on Ukrainian as the only official language, when a third of the population (at least) mainly spoke Russian; the Nazi collaborators promoted to national heroes. But that's not what is at issue now. Ukraine had not attacked us. Yet Russian missiles are striking cities like Mariupol, Kharkiv, and Odesa – Russian-speaking cities – 'defending' Russian speakers by flooring their homes into rubble.

Since this all kicked off, I've been to quite a few countries in or around Europe, and I personally haven't felt any Russophobia (I can't speak for others, but I didn't encounter it myself); in fact, the opposite. All the Ukrainians I've met knew immediately where I was from yet showed no seething rage but rather sympathy. It's almost as if the idea that Ukrainians who don't want a foreign army raping and pillaging on their soil are rabidly nationalist, Russian-hating Nazis is bullshit.

So, it's frustrating when some who call themselves anti-imperialists tell me they support Putin, either because they mistakenly believe only Israel, the United States, and on certain days Saudi Arabia can be the villains on the world stage, or they're trying to be nice, not knowing what I, as a Russian, actually think.

Against double standards

Look, I get it: as Noam Chomsky says, you should begin by fighting imperialism at home. But guess what? I'm from an empire, too, and being Russian, I'd be a hypocrite if I called out Uncle Sam and not Uncle Vlad when he does the exact same thing.

We keep hearing that NATO is a defensive alliance whose members join it willingly, but look at it from Russia's perspective: our country is almost completely surrounded by US military bases. It doesn't matter how they got there, and 'We're defensive, just trust me, bro!' doesn't exactly inspire confidence from a superpower that breaks international law faster than you can say 'WMDS'.

Washington had a similar fear of Soviet expansion in Latin America, so it staged coups, handed guns to cocaine-running counterrevolutionaries, and invaded sovereign islands to guard its sphere of influence. It was wrong then, it's wrong now, and it's still wrong when Putin does it. 'They did it, so why can't I?' is the masterful reasoning of a five-year-old.

I don't like how NATO has crept up to Russia's borders for the past thirty years. But what I like even less is three-month-old babies in Odesa being blown to pieces by Russian missiles; Odesa, by the way, a city at the heart of Russian culture, music, and literature: Odessa Mama. It's as if the Americans bombed New Orleans. Saving Russian speakers, my ass.

Even if Ukraine joined NATO, so what? Turkey is in NATO, and we get along just fine. And if other countries, like Finland, didn't want to join NATO before, they sure as hell do now. All Putin's master plan to save us from NATO encirclement by adding another 1,340 kilometres of it to our border, I suppose.

And yes, the Western powers are hypocrites: Europe was all like #refugeeswelcome, only having just let thousands of black and brown children fill the seabed. It's good that they're helping Ukrainians now, but it would have been nice to see this attitude before. Yet there are worse things to be than a hypocrite – someone who cheers on war crimes, for instance.

And then there's this framing of Russia / Ukraine as the 'civilized' Europeans vs. the barbaric Asian hordes and the pearl-clutching over how 'this' could happen in Europe. (Yugoslavia wasn't that long ago.) Russians have embraced European values since Peter the Great, and taking over land that doesn't belong to you then wiping out the natives who resist is as European as it gets. British history can be summed up as: 'This is mine. Oh, you thought this was yours? Well, where's your gunpowder, then?' These Asian-hordes tropes belong in the 1800s.

But none of this racist Western hypocrisy is a good enough reason why Ukrainian women should be raped because their husbands are 'Nazis'.

For sure, some say that all didn't happen – the horrors in Bucha and Mariupol are Western propaganda. It is curious how these hoaxes only seem to happen to the Russians and their allies and no one else. One would think Ukraine has a thriving film industry in the midst of a warzone, with thousands of extras so dedicated to their craft they'll have to stay in character the rest of their lives.

In fact, not only are they so convincing at playing dead, but they've got all their friends, relatives, and hundreds of international reporters in on the act.

This isn't World War II
Which is more likely – that for the first time in history, an invading army is behaving like they're at their grandma's

house, *or* (picture this) the country being invaded is blowing themselves up to . . . make the invaders look bad?

If you don't trust the mainstream media, why do you trust the Russian mainstream media? Would you believe the White House press secretary if she spewed that garbage? What makes Putin's spokesmen like Dmitry Peskov and foreign minister Sergey Lavrov – who won't even call it a 'war' – more trustworthy? Right until the bombs started dropping on Kyiv, the Russian government was still telling us there wouldn't be a war. Why should we believe anything that comes out of their mouths?

Lavrov in particular seems to be losing his marbles. Adolf Hitler was Jewish? The West wants to destroy Orthodox Christendom? I don't know how much more of this stupidity I can take.

What I hear from such self-styled anti-imperialists is they only care about one empire. They don't care about us in Russia and Ukraine. Why don't you show solidarity with the tens of thousands of Russians, including leftists, feminists, and anti-imperialists, who took to the streets against the war? Right now, it doesn't feel like you're on our side.

The USSR wasn't a perfect socialist utopia, but when my parents were growing up there was at least a pretence of pushing back against class and racial oppression (even if it didn't always turn out that way). That Soviet Union, which stood with Africa's liberation struggle, is dead. Putin's Russia, where a handful of his cronies hoard all the wealth, is now the opposite of whatever the USSR once stood for.

Putin is now what Bush was in 2003.

'I Marched against Putin's War' was first published on 18 July 2022 by *Jacobin*, www.jacobin.com/ 2022/07/putin-war-russia-ukraine-empire-lies

A Left Divided: Anti-War, Anti-Imperialism and the Russian Invasion of Ukraine

Gilbert Achcar

Gilbert Achcar dissects the differences as well as their origins and their outcomes.

The anti-war, anti-imperialist left worldwide has been deeply divided on the war in Ukraine along quite unusual lines, due to the novelty of the situation represented by Russia's invasion of a weaker neighbouring country as part of Russia's openly stated nationalistic expansionist ambitions, along with NATO's active and substantial support for the invaded country's resistance. The same left had already been facing division over Russia's murderous intervention in Syria after Iran's, but the conditions were very different.

Moscow intervened on behalf of the existing Syrian government, a fact that some took as a pretext to justify or excuse it. Support to Russia's military intervention in Syria or, at best, refusal to condemn it were in most cases predicated on a geopolitical one-sided 'anti-imperialism' that considered the fate of the Syrian people as subordinate to the supreme goal of opposing US-led Western imperialism seen as supportive of the Syrian uprising.

The war in Ukraine presented what looked like a simpler and more straightforward case. Russia waged a war of invasion in Ukraine similar to those waged by US imperialism in various countries since World War II, from Korea to Vietnam to Iraq and Afghanistan. But since it wasn't Washington but Moscow that was invading, and since those fighting against the invasion weren't supported by Moscow and Beijing but by Washington and its NATO allies, most of the anti-war anti-imperialist left reacted very differently.

One section of that left, taking its neo-campist single-minded opposition to US imperialism and its allies to the extreme, supported Russia, labelling it as 'anti-imperialist' by turning the concept of imperialism from one based on the critique of capitalism into one based on a quasi-cultural hatred of the West. Another section acknowledged the imperialist nature of the present Russian state but deemed it to be a lesser imperialist power that ought not to be opposed according to the logic of the 'lesser evil'.

Still another section of the anti-war anti-imperialist left, acknowledging likewise the imperialist nature of Russia's invasion of Ukraine, condemned it, and demanded that it stop. However, it fell short of supporting Ukraine's resistance to the invasion, except by piously wishing it success, while refusing to support its right to get the weapons it needs for its defence. Worse still, most of the same people oppose the delivery of such weapons by the NATO powers in a blatant subordination of the fate of the Ukrainians to the presumed 'supreme' consideration of anti-Western anti-imperialism. Or else they claim that such deliveries turn the war into an inter-imperialist war, which justifies opposing them.

There is no dispute that the Ukraine war has turned into a proxy confrontation between Russian imperialism and Western imperialist powers. Now, let us imagine that the United States invaded Venezuela, as it contemplated doing for a while under Donald Trump, and that Russia decided to supply the Venezuelan government of Nicolás Maduro with weapons to help it fight the invaders. This situation would clearly be one of a just war waged by Venezuela against a US imperialist invasion, against the background of an ongoing conflict between US imperialism and Russian imperialism.

Venezuela's just war would, therefore, be at the same time a 'proxy war' between two imperialist powers, in the same way that most conflicts during the Cold War – such as the Korean war or the Vietnam war – were wars of national liberation as well as 'proxy wars' between Washington and Moscow.

What would the right position be for internationalist anti-imperialists? Unless you are an absolute pacifist believing in 'turning the other cheek', you would support arms deliveries to the Venezuelan resistance to enable it to defend its population and achieve a position from which it could avoid capitulation and lessen the price to pay in the negotiations. If anyone said, 'We support the Venezuelan resistance, but oppose both Russian arms deliveries to the Maduro government and economic pressure on the United States,' this attitude would rightly be regarded as not serious.

For such a position would be proclaiming support to the Venezuelans while depriving them of the means to resist and opposing that economic pressure be put on their aggressor. At best, this would be an utterly inconsistent position. At worst, a hypocritical position disguising an indifference to the fate of the Venezuelans – seen as sacrificial lambs on the altar of anti-imperialism (Russian imperialism in this case) – behind a pretence of wishing them success in their just resistance.

This bring us to the key distinction between a direct war between imperialist countries in which every side is trying to grab a part of the world, as was most classically the case in World War I, and an invasion by an imperialist power of a non-imperialist country, where the latter is backed by another imperialist power using it as a proxy in inter-imperialist rivalry.

In the first case, working-class internationalism requires that workers, including workers in uniform (i.e., soldiers), oppose the war on both sides, each opposing their own government's war, even if that would contribute to its defeat (this is the meaning of 'revolutionary defeatism'). In the second case, revolutionary defeatism is required only from workers and soldiers who belong to the aggressor imperialist country, and in a much more active way than indirectly. They are required to sabotage their country's war machine. Workers of the oppressed nation, on the other hand, have every right and duty to defend their country and families and must be supported by internationalists worldwide. It is through the angle of such practical consequences of political positions that the attitude towards the ongoing war must be defined.

The most hypocritical iteration of the refusal to support the Ukrainians' right to defend themselves and get the means they need for that has consisted in feigning concern for them by representing them as being used by NATO as cannon fodder in a proxy inter-imperialist war. Hence, a phony show of pity for the Ukrainians depicted as being cynically sent weapons by NATO powers so that they carry on fighting until total exhaustion. This allows those expressing such views to oppose NATO governments' delivery of defensive weapons to the Ukrainians in the guise of humanistic concerns about them.

This fake sympathy, however, totally obliterates the Ukrainians' agency, to the point of contradicting the most obvious: not a single day has passed since the Russian invasion began without the Ukrainian president publicly blaming NATO powers for not sending enough weapons, both quantitatively and qualitatively. If NATO imperialist powers were cynically using the Ukrainians to drain their Russian imperialist rival, as that type of incoherent analysis would have it, they would certainly not need to be begged to send more weapons.

The truth is that key NATO powers – not least among them France and Germany, both of them major suppliers of weapons to Ukraine – are eager to see the war stop. Although the war has substantial benefits to their military industrial complexes, such specific sectors' gains are far outweighed by the overall impact of looming energy shortages, rising inflation, massive refugee crisis, and disruption to the international capitalist system as a whole, at a time of global political uncertainty and rise of the far right.

Finally, there is a section of the global anti-war anti-imperialist left that rejects the provision of weapons to the Ukrainians in the name of peace, advocating negotiations as an alternative to war. One could believe that we were back to the time of the Vietnam war, when the anti-war movement was split between pro-Moscow Communist Parties who advocated peace and the radical left that openly wished for Vietnam's victory against the US invasion. The situation today is quite different, however. At the time of Vietnam, both wings of the anti-war movement were in full solidarity with the Vietnamese. Both supported the Vietnamese's right to acquire weapons for their defence. Their disagreement was tactical, about which slogan to put forward in order to most effectively build an anti-war movement that could help Vietnam in its national struggle.

Today, on the other hand, those who advocate 'peace' while opposing the Ukrainians' right to acquire weapons for their defence are counterposing peace to fighting. In other words, they are wishing for the capitulation of Ukraine – for which 'peace' could have resulted if the Ukrainians had not been armed and hence not been able to defend their country? We could have been writing 'Order prevails in Kyiv!' today, but that would have been the New Order forced by Moscow on the Ukrainian nation under the most deceitful pretext of 'denazification'.

Negotiations are going on between Kyiv and Moscow, under the aegis of NATO member, Turkey. So, it is certainly not like some side is refusing to negotiate. Now, it doesn't take much expertise in war history to understand that negotiations depend on the balance of forces achieved on the ground. The ongoing negotiations won't lead to a peace treaty except in one of two ways. One is that Ukraine will no longer be able to carry on fighting and will have to capitulate and accept Moscow's diktat, even if this diktat has been considerably watered down from Putin's initially stated goals due to the heroic resistance of the Ukrainian armed forces and population. The second possibility is that Russia will no longer be able to carry on fighting, either militarily because of the moral exhaustion of its troops, or economically because of widespread dissatisfaction among the Russian population – in the same way that, in World War I, the difficulties encountered by Czarist Russia's troops and the economic consequences of the war on the Russian population led the latter to rise up and bring Czarism down in 1917. A similar cause led to the failed 1905 Revolution in the wake of Russia's defeat in its war against Japan.

True internationalists, anti-war advocates, and anti-imperialists can only be wholeheartedly in favour of the second scenario. They must, therefore, support the Ukrainians' right to get the weapons they need for their defence. Supporting Ukraine's position in negotiations about its own national territory requires a support to its resistance and its right to acquire the weapons that are necessary for its defence from whichever source possesses such weapons and is willing to provide them. Refusing Ukraine's right to acquire such weapons is basically a call for it to capitulate. In the face of an overwhelmingly armed and most brutal invader, this is actually defeatism on the wrong side, virtually amounting to support for the invader.

'A Left Divided' was first published in June 2022 by the *Scottish Left Review*, www.scottishleftreview.scot/anti-war-and-anti-imperialism

Why is Ukrainian Resistance Invisible to You? An Appeal to Supporters of the Stop the War Coalition

Simon Pirani

Here are notes I made for a talk at an on-line meeting of the Stop the War Coalition's Brent (north-west London) branch tomorrow (28 June 2022). I was due to speak alongside Lindsey German, national convenor of the STWC. But last week it turned out that she had an unavoidable clash, no one else was available, and the event was cancelled.

I wrote to Brent STWC to say that I thought the cancellation was 'a shame, politically speaking', because there have been 'precious few meaningful exchanges of views between those in the UK labour movement who have a broadly "plague-on-both-your-houses" view, such as Lindsey German, and those who believe support should be given to the Ukrainian resistance, such as myself'.

An opportunity for discussion has been missed – while the biggest war in Europe since the middle of the last century rages.

Hello, thank you for inviting me.

I will start with a confession. When approached about this meeting, I was asked, as someone who has been travelling to both Russia and Ukraine for a long time, whether I could put Brent Stop the War in touch with a suitable Ukrainian speaker. I said I could not think of anyone, but that I could do it. In fact, I would have felt embarrassed, even ashamed, to ask a Ukrainian friend to speak here.

I imagined Ukrainian friends, who daily witness the most horrendous violence against their country, looking at the coalition's web site. I thought that they would feel that here was an organization utterly removed from Ukrainian reality. An organization that – unlike some significant Russian anti-war organizations – is interested neither in Ukrainian communities' suffering, nor in those communities' response to that suffering. An organization that seems uncritically to accept, and even repeat, Russian government propaganda.

I am not trying to speak for Ukrainians. I am explaining why I would hesitate to ask them to break off from the life and death issues they are dealing with, to interact with an organization that appears unable to address the causes of their grief.

I will talk about four political issues related to the war, and finish up with some practical suggestions, as I have been asked to do.

1   The Ukrainian population

The Ukrainian population, which is both combatant and victim in the war, is literally invisible on the Stop the War web site. I know that Stop the War is a coalition, but the site is its public face, and the Ukrainian population is invisible there.

President Putin said on the first day of the invasion that he expected Ukrainians to greet the Russian troops with flowers, and sections of the Ukrainian armed forces to revolt. Why did these things not happen? In my view it's because most Ukrainians support the resistance to a one-sided, aggressive war, in which the Russian army is targeting civilians with massacres, rapes and executions. They do not see it as a war of two equal sides.

Real Ukrainians fighting in volunteer units, or medical or transport workers risking their lives, or Ukrainians in

London raising money for bullet-proof vests, are invisible in the imaginary Stop the War world. There, they are only 'NATO proxies'. But that world bears no relation to the Ukraine they live in, or have migrated from.

Here is a question to Lindsey German. In May last year, you wrote that Stop the War is 'supporting the people of Palestine, who have a right to resist occupation'. I agree with that. But why no such statement about Ukraine?

And if Ukrainians, or Palestinians, have a right to resist, what does it mean? Does it only mean standing up to tanks with your bare hands, as Ukrainians have had to do? Does it mean throwing stones, often the only weapons that young Palestinians have? What about proper weapons? Do you think Palestinians have a right to those? And Ukrainians?

I don't think these are easy questions to answer. But if we don't acknowledge a right to resist, we won't even be asking them. And anyone's attitude to stopping the war in Ukraine, or the war against Palestine or any other war, is bound to be shaped by their attitude to this right to resistance.

2   This is an imperialist war of aggression

Russia is in the second rank of imperialist powers, and part of the driving force of its militarism is to make up for economic weakness. Nevertheless, it is an imperial power. There is no mention of this on the Stop the War web site.

On the contrary, there are indications that prominent spokespeople for Stop the War think that Putin has a point, when he talks about re-integrating Russia's old colonies into what he calls the 'Russian world'.

For example, Andrew Murray, writing on the web site, quoted Putin's historical article about Russia and Ukraine published last summer. Murray picked out an assertion by Putin that he said he agreed with: that, with the collapse of the Soviet Union, 'all those territories, and, which is more important, people, found themselves abroad overnight, taken away from their historical motherland'.

When Putin speaks about Russia being the 'historical motherland', it sends chills down the spines not only of Ukrainians, but of people in the Caucasus and central Asia whose countries were forcibly incorporated into the Russian empire in the 19th century, and in the Baltic states, which after some decades of independence were re-incorporated into the Soviet Union under a secret agreement between Stalin and Hitler. It's maybe similar to the feeling Irish people would get, if British politicians were to tell them that Ireland is part of a historical British motherland.

To embrace this rhetoric is to embrace great-power chauvinism. What does that have to do with stopping any war anywhere?

Many wars, including this one, have some elements of people's war and some elements of inter-state conflict. In the Stop the War coalition, the idea that Ukrainians are fighting a proxy war for NATO is very widespread. But why, then, does no one suggest that, in some respects, Palestinians are fighting a proxy war for some of the Arab states? Would that invalidate their right to resist Israeli apartheid? No. One could argue that in the 1960s and 1970s, the Vietnamese were in some respects fighting a proxy war for the Soviet Union and China. Did this invalidate their resistance? No.

3   This war started in 2014

The full-scale invasion of Ukraine in February enlarged a war, waged by Russia from 2014, in which 17,000 people died and millions were driven from their homes. The Stop the War coalition did not oppose that war.

That war followed the overthrow of president Yanukovich of Ukraine by mass protests. The character of these protests continues to be fiercely debated. They were messy and complicated, and there is no doubt that fascists were active in them, as were vast numbers of other people.

Within weeks, separatists in eastern Ukraine began an armed insurgency, supported by a Russian army invasion.

From any working class or socialist point of view, Ukraine in 2014 had plenty of problems. The tensions in the eastern regions, cynically played on by politicians there, was one of these. But nothing made things worse, more quickly, than the Russian military action.

Why did Stop the War not oppose this invasion? Partly, I presume, it was influenced by the argument in Andrew Murray's article that I mentioned. It's a travesty. Murray claims that Yanukovich was overthrown by a coup, which is absurd and untrue – it was a mass movement, whether you, or I, like that movement or not. Murray paints in sympathetic colours the separatists, although their leaders were strongly influenced by extreme Russian nationalism and fascism from the start.

But most harmfully and deceitfully, Murray did not even mention the main factor that turned civil conflict into war: Russia's military action. Another invisible.

Stop the War did not oppose this Russian imperial adventure. Furthermore, in 2016, the coalition went out of its way to support the Russian political commentator Boris Kagarlitsky on the grounds that he was an 'anti-war activist', despite the fact that – in contrast to many Russian socialists and trade unionists – he wholeheartedly supported the military action.

I wrote an open letter to Stop the War, asking why you supported a warmonger. I emailed every single executive member individually. I received no response at all. I ask here that the executive review the letter and answer it. It remains relevant. If you cannot tell the difference between warmongers and anti-war activists, you will never effectively oppose any war.

The final point about 2014 is the nightmare being lived by those Ukrainians in the areas occupied by Russia then. Half the population had left by 2017. The regimes that governed those who remained were lawless and dictatorial, destroying labour rights and civil rights. Knowledge of the hardship and brutality in those areas has been a motivation for Ukrainians resisting Russian occupation in other eastern regions.

4 Russia and the Western powers

If the Stop the War coalition takes war seriously, it will engage in a serious discussion about the issue of NATO expansion. According to some of Stop the War's spokespeople, this is a cause – even, the main cause – of the war in Ukraine. And since NATO expansion, together with so called 'denazification', were the Kremlin's main pretexts for the full-scale invasion of Ukraine in February, this is a live political issue.

The idea that Russia feels threatened by NATO moving to its borders is repeated in many articles on the Stop the War web site. But obviously, in the real world, things are not so simple. (1) Russia has had NATO countries on its borders since 2004. (2) Ukraine has never had a NATO membership action plan. And public support for joining NATO was very low, until Russia invaded in 2014. Cause and effect are mixed up, time and time again, in the articles you publish.

Are you, as supporters of Stop the War, serious about analysing relationships between different imperialist countries? The focus on NATO expansion is based on a misreading of the actual dynamic between Russia and the NATO powers. Those powers supported the murderous Russian assault on Chechnya with which Putin began his presidency. Then, whatever their public statements, they treated the Putin regime as a gendarme that would control its own sphere of influence.

This included Georgia, which Russia invaded in 2008. It included Syria, where Russia, tolerated by the Western powers, militarily supported the massacre of civilians by the Assad government in 2016 – another slaughter that was largely invisible for Stop the War.

This tacit alliance between the Western powers and the Kremlin has been broken by the full-scale invasion of

Ukraine this year. But that cannot be understood on the basis of such a one-sided view of what went before.

Practical points

I have been asked to point to practical things that people could do about the war. The things that I believe make sense are not about state policy, but in the sphere of civil society and the labour movement.

First, French, Austrian and other trade unions have organized convoys of material and medical aid to Ukrainian communities. I think such initiatives are valuable.

The Confederation of Free Trade Unions of Ukraine, which supports workers' organizations in conflict areas, and territorial defence units, also welcomes this type of support from outside Ukraine.

An initiative that I have participated in is seeking ways for civil society and labour organizations outside Ukraine to help support Ukrainians in the Russian-occupied territories. We have two public zoom calls coming up, with Ukrainian activists, about this. I invite people to join.

Here in the UK, as well as supporting refugees, as I am sure many people here do, I suggest following what Ukrainian organizations are doing. Here in London, we have the Ukrainian Institute, which runs a first-class programme of informational and education events. Listening to Ukrainians, and becoming well-informed, would be good steps to take.

'Why is Ukrainian Resistance Invisible to You?' was first published in June 2022 by *People and Nature*, www.peopleandnature.wordpress.com/2022/06/27/why-is-ukrainian-resistance-invisible-to-you

Ukraine and the Peace Movement

Stephen R. Shalom and Dan La Botz

It is urgent to end the war in Ukraine. But to achieve this goal, 'Russia Out Now' is a better slogan than 'Diplomacy Now'.

The global peace movement has in general an admirable history of opposing wars that have caused so much suffering over the years. Activists have championed peace and social justice from Vietnam to Central America to Iraq, helping teach the world that in place of death and destruction, xenophobia and intolerance, we can work to resolve conflicts peacefully while devoting our efforts to meeting real human needs. The peace movement has long pointed out the gargantuan waste represented by spending on war. If all the money spent on weapons of death had been redirected towards human needs, poverty and hunger could have been wiped out long ago.

And so, given our admiration and appreciation for the peace movement, we have been disappointed and a little surprised to find ourselves at odds on the question of Ukraine with people with whom in the past we have frequently marched for peace.

Here's where we agree with the peace movement. First, we both oppose Vladimir Putin's invasion and occupation of regions of Ukraine. We agree that Ukraine is an independent nation and that Russia is the aggressor. Second, we both sympathize with the soldiers and civilians who are dying and being displaced or forced into exile by this war.

Third, we both oppose militarism and war and understand that NATO – while not directly responsible for this war – also represents a problem because it is a military alliance. In the early 1990s, with the fall of the Soviet Union, new structures of mutual security should have been built instead of expanding Washington's Cold War alliance.

Having this much in common, we should be able to have a fruitful discussion and perhaps find ways to engage in some common actions. Our ability to discuss these matters does not, however, extend to those who have excused or even supported Russia, or who, ignoring Russia's primary responsibility for the aggression, want to blame the United States or NATO or the European Union for the war. Their support for Russia excludes them both from the peace movement and from the call for international solidarity with the victims of aggression.

The peace movement, it seems to us, has made three arguments for its demands for diplomacy and peace now. First, US support of weapons for Ukraine prolongs the war. Second, the provision of arms takes money from the US budget that would otherwise be allocated to important social programmes in the areas of housing, education, social welfare, and the environment. Third, the Ukraine war threatens to disrupt grain production and distribution and, by reducing supply and causing a rise in prices, will lead to mass hunger in the Middle East, North Africa, and other regions of the Global South. Let's look at each of these arguments in turn.

Militarism and war

In considering the argument that aid to Ukraine promotes militarism and war, the starting point has to be: 'Do you believe that a country that has been unjustly attacked has the right to defend itself?' If so, and if the country lacks the means to defend itself, is it entitled to receive arms from outside? Though the peace movement wants a world in which no disputes are settled by war, until such a world exists it cannot deny other peoples, such as the Ukrainians, the right of self-defence.

Some in the peace movement, of course, are absolute pacifists who believe that war is always wrong and counter-productive, even in cases of self-defence. Much of what pacifists say about war is extremely valuable: they note the long-term costs that are often left out of the cost-benefit analyses of the decision to take up arms, among them the regimentation of societies at war, the inevitable civilian deaths, and the brutalized sensibilities that afflict even the most virtuous warriors. Most of us in the peace movement are not absolute pacifists. We generally believe that, even acknowledging these costs, there are still times when military resistance against an aggressor is justified. Absolute pacifists disagree, but it would be extremely unlikely that even a pacifist who believed in justice would denounce someone for providing arms to a victim of aggression. So, there is no reason why the peace movement should attack the provision of arms to Ukraine.

Some pacifists call upon victims of aggression to use non-violent civil disobedience or other means to resist. To be sure, civilian resistance and other forms of nonviolent resistance can be much more effective than commonly believed, and it is right for the peace movement to make this point and advocate for such policies. But it seems inappropriate for outsiders to tell Ukrainians *as the bombs are falling* that they must use only nonviolence or raise the white flag and surrender.

The peace movement believes in peace, but of course it doesn't consider peace to be the only value. That's why many peace organizations list peace and justice as their joint missions. Historically, the great majority of peace forces concluded that, while failing to resist Hitler's armies might have led to peace, it would not have led to a better world. Likewise, at the time of the US Civil War, acquiescing in the Confederacy's secession would have secured peace but at the expense of the continuing horrors of slavery. In the case of Ukraine, war causes great harm to social justice along many dimensions. But surrender – for that is what peace at any cost means – also causes terrible harm to social justice. Putin has said he would eliminate Ukraine as a nation and the Ukrainians as a people, arguing that they are part of Russia. He wishes to conquer Ukraine and bring it under his authoritarian rule, in a society without democracy or civil liberties. So we ask, war or surrender? Which causes more harm? Can outsiders really judge that for Ukrainians?

The peace movement didn't in the name of peace call for the Soviet Union or China to stop providing arms to North Vietnam, or for Eastern European Communist nations to discontinue the provision of weapons to the Sandinistas in the 1980s. Leftists and liberals didn't consider the Western denial of weapons to the Spanish Republic in the 1930s an expression of peace but a failure of political will on the part of the democratic nations, if not a disguised sympathy for Franco.

In the past, of course, we have often opposed arms exports because they prop up human-rights-abusing regimes. But in this case, the weapons are an attempt to assist a people who have been unjustly attacked in defending themselves, just as was the aim of Lend-Lease to Britain and the USSR during World War II.

Some might argue that Vietnam and Republican Spain were progressive governments, while Ukraine is corrupt or even fascist. We believe that the character of the government is not the key issue, but rather the fact that it is engaged in a justified anti-imperialist struggle of national self-determination. When from 1935 to 1937 Italy made war on Ethiopia, most of the Left supported the latter even though Emperor Haile Selassie's government was authoritarian and reactionary. The Left did so because it was important to support a sovereign nation against Italian Fascist imperialism, a regime that by 1936 was allied with Nazi Germany. The essence of the position is anti-imperialism and the defence of self-determination.

The case of Ukraine, however, is much easier to decide. Ukraine, which has had problems with foreign meddling from all sides and entrenched corruption, is fundamentally a democratic country, with leaders who have been replaced in elections. There are civil liberties, though undoubtedly under threat, especially under conditions of war. Like other nations around the world, it has a far right and neo-Nazi organizations, among them the notorious Azov regiment. These forces, however, have fared poorly in elections and do not control President Volodymyr Zelenskiy's neoliberal government. Within Ukraine, there is a legal, democratic socialist left that some of us in the US Left have been supporting.

While we believe Ukraine has the right to get arms wherever it can to defend itself, we recognize that the direct involvement of the United States or NATO could lead either to a broader European war or to the use of nuclear arms. We should be vigilant and oppose any such development. And, if things get to the point where the Zelenskiy government is continuing the war contrary to the wishes of the Ukrainian population, then it would right for outsiders to object to shipping further arms. But polls – limited as they are in time of war – suggest that this is not currently the case.

Many on the Left have suggested that Washington is pursuing a 'proxy war' against Russia and that it is pushing the Ukrainians to 'fight until the last Ukrainian'. Of course, the United States would like to see a weakened Russia, but it is hardly the case that the Ukrainians are persevering only because of US pressure. The Ukrainians fight of their own volition, and the United States cannot make them fight, though it could force them to surrender by refusing them arms. Indeed, it is clear that the Biden administration and other Western leaders are quite worried about the economic consequences of a long war and the risks to their other geopolitical interests.

Arms for Ukraine and social spending

Long before Russia invaded Ukraine, the Biden administration found its congressional support too narrow to pass its social programme. Holding a bare majority in the Senate, the Democrats could not overcome the undemocratic filibuster and the defections of one or two right-wing Democrats. Biden's programme has also suffered because of former president Donald Trump's tax cuts and the failure of the Democrats to restore the higher tax rates on corporations and the wealthy.

A progressive tax policy could easily fund Build Back Better *and* arms to Ukraine. Aid to Ukraine would not have affected a single vote in Congress regarding Build Back Better.

Some us peace movement activists have criticized progressives in Congress for voting for military and economic aid to Ukraine while their social agenda (for a Green New Deal or Medicare for All) has yet to be addressed. But the support for Ukraine from congressional progressives has not led them to abandon their social agenda. Nor is it the case that, but for the Ukraine aid, the Green New Deal and other progressive legislation would have been enacted. us spending on arms for Ukraine has had absolutely no impact on the country's social budget, though it might if the war continues long enough or expands.

Hunger in the global South

The peace movement is also rightly concerned about the impact of the Ukraine war on the supply of food to Africa and other parts of the global South. As one of the world's leading grain producers, Ukraine has seen its shipments blocked by fighting in agricultural areas, and Russian troops have burned fields and attacked Ukrainian grain elevators and ports. True, if Ukraine were to surrender tomorrow, grain exports – limited by the damage already done by the war – could be resumed. But of course, if Russia ceased its military onslaught and withdrew its invading forces, grain exports could also be resumed.

To prevent the horrendous consequences of Russian aggression for the people of the Third World, should the peace movement call for Ukraine to sue for peace and likely lose its sovereignty? No, it should call for Russia to end the war and withdraw from Ukraine. If it does not, we should pursue other ways of getting food to those in need. For example, we could call upon the United Nations General Assembly to use its power under the Uniting for Peace resolution (which is not subject to veto) to escort grain ships to and from Ukrainian ports. We should *not* call for unilateral action by the United States to protect grain shipments, which could be seen as a provocation. But a UN-authorized humanitarian escort would be quite different. Insurance carriers might be reluctant to cover vessels sailing into the Black Sea, but the European Union could offer the coverage. The key principle here is this: the peace movement should not demand that Ukraine give up its freedom because Russia is holding the global South's food supplies hostage when other less onerous solutions are available.

The question of diplomacy

The peace movement has a standard position in favour of diplomacy over war. But think about the Vietnam war. While many liberal opponents of the war called for 'Negotiations Now', the demand of the radical anti-war movement – made up of millions who marched in the streets – was 'Out Now.' Their point was that the United States had no moral rights in Vietnam and therefore there was nothing for it to negotiate. It needed simply to withdraw its troops. The radicals knew, of course, that despite the demands of justice, the United States was unlikely to simply pick up and leave and that there would be negotiations. We also knew that Vietnam would negotiate, and we wouldn't criticize them for doing so – it was their call – but we also understood that what happened on the battlefield would affect the outcome of any negotiations. So, while we wanted peace, we supported Vietnam's struggle for independence against the United States.

The same is true in Ukraine today. Justice demands immediate and unconditional Russian withdrawal from all of Ukraine. Russian anti-war activists have also taken this position. We say to Russia as we once said to the United States: 'Out Now!'

In fact, like nearly all wars, this one will almost certainly end in some sort of negotiated agreement. But the nature of that agreement – whether the Ukrainian people will be able to continue to exist as an independent and sovereign nation – will depend on the military situation there. This in turn will depend on the political situation and the degree of solidarity with Ukraine throughout the world. Without foreign arms, Ukraine will be forced to accept a horrible agreement that could dismember the country or even end its independent existence and democratic government. With arms, they can win the war, reclaim all of their territory, and defend their democratic government or, if not, reach a settlement they find acceptable. Is the death and destruction that will ensue worth it? How can that be a decision of anyone but the people of Ukraine?

We share the peace movement's desire to end militarism and war and to dismantle military alliances and end the threat of nuclear annihilation. NATO should be dismantled and replaced with treaties guaranteeing respect for national sovereignty and reducing military bases and arms. Wealthy nations like the United States, China, Japan, and the European Union have a responsibility to ensure that the Global South is free from hunger. With all of this in common, let's open a genuine dialogue on the question of Ukraine's right to self-determination and self-defence within the context of establishing a world that is more democratic, more equal, and more secure for all.

'Ukraine and the Peace Movement' was first published on 19 July 2022 by *Foreign Policy in Focus*, www.fpif.org/ukraine-and-the-peace-movement

About the Ukraine Solidarity Campaign

The Ukraine Solidarity Campaign seeks to organize solidarity and provide information in support of Ukrainian socialists and trade unionists, campaigning for working class and democratic rights, against imperialist intervention and national chauvinism. It seeks to co-ordinate socialist and labour movement organizations who agree on this task, regardless of differences and opinions on other questions.

Basic aims of the Ukraine Solidarity Campaign are:

- to support and build direct links with the independent socialists and the labour movement in Ukraine.
- to support the right of the Ukrainian people to determine their own future free from external intervention from Russian or Western imperialism.

The Ukraine Solidarity Campaign collaborates with the European Network for Solidarity with Ukraine, www.ukraine-solidarity.eu

Supporters of Ukraine Solidarity Campaign include:

- Associated Society of Locomotive Engineers and Firemen
- National Union of Mineworkers
- Public and Commercial Services Union
- Anti-Capitalist Resistance
- Alliance for Workers Liberty
- The Real Democracy Movement
- Republican Socialist Platform
- International Marxist-Humanist Organisation
- Independent Socialists in Wellingborough

Contact the Ukraine Solidarity Campaign:
ukrainesolidaritycampaign@gmail.com
www.ukrainesolidaritycampaign.org

About Resistance Books

Resistance Books is a radical publisher of internationalist, ecosocialist, and feminist books. We publish books in collaboration with the International Institute for Research and Education in Amsterdam (www.iire.org). For further information, including a full list of titles available and how to order them, go to the Resistance Books website.

info@resistancebooks.org
www.resistancebooks.org